Jón Hnefill Aðalste

A PIECE OF HORSE LIVER

MYTH, RITUAL AND FOLKLORE
IN OLD ICELANDIC SOURCES

Translated by

Terry Gunnell
and
Joan Turville-Petre

Háskólaútgáfan
Félagsvísindastofnun
Reykjavík 1998

A PIECE OF HORSE LIVER
Myth, Ritual and Folklore in Old Icelandic Sources
© 1998 Jón Hnefill Aðalsteinsson
           Háskólaútgáfan
           Félagsvísindastofnun

Hönnun kápu: Dægradvöl
Umbrot: Guðmundur Þorsteinsson
Prentumsjón: PMS
Bókband: Bókavirkið

ISBN 9979-54-264-0

A PIECE OF HORSE LIVER

Content

Foreword

THE ARTICLES in this book are all based on lectures that were presented at foreign universities or conferences. They have all been previously published in foreign and Icelandic books and journals (six in English and two in Icelandic), but since these works are somewhat scattered, if not difficult to get hold of, it was thought fitting to republish them in a special book. Minor alterations have been made to update the texts where neccessary and applicable. Furthermore, additional footnotes contain brief comments about the most recent ideas to have appeared with regard to the subject material of each individual article, and about the reactions that the articles provoked when they were originally published. The *Introduction* deals briefly with the same things, and draws attention to particular innovatory research where such research is relevant and available.

Háskólaútgáfan University Press and The Social Science Institute have gone out of their way to prepare these articles for republication in the best possible fashion. I would like to express my gratitude to Professor Stefán Ólafsson, the Director of the Social Science Institute, and Jörundur Guðmundsson, the Executive Director of Háskólaútgáfan University Press for accepting these articles as readily as they did. I would also like to thank Dr Friðrik H. Jónsson for his positive reaction when the subject of this publication first came up, and Ingibjörg Ásta Gunnarsdóttir for her assistance with typing. I am also grateful to Guðmundur Þorsteinsson for his careful work on the setting of the book.

Six of the articles in this book have been translated into English by Joan Turville-Petre, B. Litt. M.A. The two remaining articles have been translated by Dr Terry Gunnell, lecturer in Folkloristics, who has also translated the foreword, introduction, and Postscript, and has been responsible for various comments and other small changes that have been made in the text of the articles in this republication in addition to reading over the proofs. I would like to express my gratitude to both of these translators for their hard work.

Last but not least I would like to thank my wife, Svava Jakobs-dóttir, A.B. in Literature, for her supportive and critical reading from the time at which these articles first came into being until they were finally assembled for this book.

Jón Hnefill Aðalsteinsson

as possible. The Nordic gods play little part in the *fornaldarsögur* and there are few real stories about gods and giants to be found here. The *fornaldarsögur*, therefore, have little relevance for the present investigation into the relations between the gods and giants at the time of the Old Norse religion. Apart from that, these stories must be considered as being very dubious and untrustworthy sources of information with regard to the giants themselves. They, too, must be used with the utmost caution in this connection.[5]

Many Scandinavian folk tales mention the giants, or trolls, but the picture here is even more exaggerated than that found in the *fornaldarsögur*. In many of those tales that deal with the giants, it is stated specifically that these beings existed in the far distant past, but died out long before the time of the story itself. This probably represents a faint memory of the giants having left the field long ago, perhaps at a similar time to the Nordic gods, or at the time of the Conversion. Indeed, many folk tales about the giants illustrate the giants' dislike for churches, and particularly for the sound of bells which are said to have frightened them away from their original native habitat.[6]

In the light of what has been said above about source material, the mythological poems of the Edda have to be considered the most valuable sources of information on the giants in Old Norse mythology, and the relations between the giants and the gods. Next come the poems of Egill Skalla-Grímsson and those other named poets of the ninth and tenth centuries who refer to these subjects in their works. Snorri's *Prose Edda* comes in third place, followed by the *fornaldarsögur* and finally the later-day folk tales.

Certain scholars who have written about the *jǫtnar* in the past take a different view of the sources to that taken here. C. W. von Sydow, for example, writes in his essay, "Jätterna i mytologi och folktro":

> Då det gäller att utforska våra förfäders jätteförställningar, er det därför bäst att ej gå direkt till Eddadiktingen, utan att först se efter vad slags jätteföreställningar som träffas i den rena folktraditionen; och sedan man där gjort sig förtrogen med de olikea type-

---

5 Sigurður Nordal 1953, 228 ff.: Einar Ól. Sveinsson 1959, 499-507 and references.
6 von Sydow 1919, 52-96 and references.

rna, se till vilka motsvarigheter som träffas i Eddan. Då blir det också lätt att bedöma det stoff som ej erbjuder någon direkt motsvarighet till folktraditionen. Det är denna väg jag här skal försöka att gå.[7]

(With regard to our forefathers' beliefs concerning the giants, it is thus best not to go directly to the poems of the Edda, but to instead first consider the kinds of beliefs encountered in pure folk tradition; and when we have become well aquainted with various different types, we can examine the comparative features found in the Edda. Then it will also become quite easy to judge the material that has no direct parallel in folk tradition. This is the route I mean to follow.)

The emphasis von Sydow places here on the oral tradition and folk tales as primary sources of material on the giants, as opposed to the mythological poems of the Edda, has lent support to the creation of an academic view of the giants which is somewhat different to that actually preserved in the mythological poems and the scaldic poetry of the tenth century. Amongst others, this applies to Jan de Vries who, in his *Altgermanische Religionsgeschichte*, takes particular note of von Sydow's argument, writing first and foremost about the giants of folk tale and legend, and only later going on to deal with the giants of the mythological poems of the Edda.[8] This attitude to the source material on the giants has come to be relatively widespread.[9]

Family Relationships between the Gods and Giants

Several references are made in the Eddic poems to a family relationship between the gods and the giants. According to the *Prose Edda*, Óðinn is the son of Bestla, the daughter of a giant named Bǫlþorn who is also mentioned in *Hávamál* (st. 140).[10] As regards Óðinn's father, Borr, the Eddic poems offer us very little information: he is mentioned in *Vǫluspá* (st. 4) and *Vǫluspá hin skamma* ("The short Vǫluspá", st. 2), but in both cases simply as the father of

---

7   von Sydow 1919, 72.
8   de Vries 1956, 241-252.
9   Halvorsen in *KLNM* VIII 1962, 693-697.
10   *Snorra-Edda* 1935, 24; *Edda,* 1987, 11.

fagnafundr	the prize that Frigg's
Friggjar niðja	progeny found,
ár borinn	borne of old
ór Jǫtunheimum[28]	from Jǫtunheimr.

The god Njǫrðr also had a wife named Skaði who was the daughter of the giant, Þjazi. They found it difficult to live together, and in one source, it is stated that Óðinn married Skaði after she left Njǫrðr.[29] In addition to this, according to the *Prose Edda*, Þórr is said to have had his son Magni with the giantess Járnsaxa.[30]

At the same time, the giants are often described as trying to gain the favours of the goddesses. In *Þrymskviða*, for example, Þrymr demands Freyja for his wife in return returning back Þórr's hammer (*Þrymskviða*, st. 8), and the giant who builds the fortifications for the Æsir demands the Sun, the Moon and Freyja as payment for his work.[31] Yet another myth tells of how the giant, Þjazi, kidnapped Iðunn and her apples, and bore them home to Jǫtunheimr.[32]

In all the aforementioned examples of relationships between the gods and giants, the two races are spoken of as equals. The first move is consistently made by the male gods and giants, and the reactions of the goddesses and giant daughters to these demands for their affections are very similar. Freyja, for example, finds the idea of marrying the giant Þrymr totally out of the question, snorting so loudly that the halls of the Æsir tremble and her necklace Brísingamen bursts. As she says,

mik veizt verða	I'd be known as
vergjarnasta,	the maddest for men
ef ek ek með þér	if I drove with you
i Jǫtunheima.[33]	to Jǫtunheimr

---

28 *Sonatorrek* sts 1 and 2, *ÍF* II, 251-252; translation based on that made by Bernard Scudder in *The Complete Sagas of Icelanders* 1997, I, 146-147.
29 Snorri Sturluson 1941, 21.
30 *Snorra-Edda*, 1935, 134; *Edda*, 1987, 79,156.
31 *Snorra-Edda*, 1935, 65; *Edda*, 1987, 35.
32 *Snorra-Edda*, 1935, 106-107; *Edda*, 1987, 60.
33 *Þrymskviða*, st. 13; *Sæmundar-Edda. Eddukvæði* 1926, 134.

The reaction of Gerðr Gymisdóttir to Freyr's suit is very alike. However, her words are nothing but polite when she is finally persuaded to accept Freyr's courtship:

þó hafðak ætlat	I little thought
at myndak aldrigi	that I would ever
unna vaningja vel.[34]	love one of the Vanir well.

Old Norse Cosmology

The giants play a large role in the Old Norse cosmology. *Vǫluspá* (st. 3), for example, talks of

| Ár var alda, | The start of time, |
| þar er Ymir byggði[35] | when Ymir lived |

even before the world is created in Ginnungagap. Óðinn and his brothers later form the world out of Ymir's body, something about which we are given more information in *Vafþrúðnismál* (st. 21) and *Grímnismál* (st. 41). The original being, Aurgelmir, father of both gods and giants is created when a drop of venom spurts out of the Élivágur rivers, and grows immediately into a giant, as is described in *Vafþrúðnismál* (st. 31). "Thence our kin came together," says Vafþrúðnir to Óðinn.

This element of similarity between the gods and the giants implies a god-like quality to the giants, who nonetheless retain their close links with nature. It might be interesting to look a little more closely at this feature, and in particular with regard to the god/giant of the wind portrayed in *Vafþrúðnismál* and elsewhere, a figure that deserves greater attention than he has so far received.

When Óðinn has asked about the creation of the earth and the origin of the first being, or oldest of the giants, he proceeds to question Vafþrúðnir about the wind which "travels invisible across the sea", as he puts it ("...ferr vág yfir; /æ menn hann sjálfan um sjá": *Vafþrúðnismál*, st. 36).

---

34 *Skírnismál*, st. 37; *Sæmundar-Edda. Eddukvæði* 1926, 91.
35 *Eddadigte* I 1962, 1.

Vafþrúðnir answers:

Hræsvelgr heitir,	Hræsvelgr he is called,
er sitr á himins enda,	he sits at the end of the sky
jǫtunn í arnar ham.	a giant in eagle form.
Af hans vængjum	They say his wings
kveða vind koma	create the wind that
alla menn yfir.[36]	fares over all humankind.

It is worth noting here that the giant who controls the wind is described as sitting in the sky, or heavens. He is in the guise of an eagle, and the rush of air caused by the movement of his wings crosses the sea in particular, since the sea and sky are the subject of this particular question and answer. These points should be borne in mind when attempting to shed light on the actual nature and characteristics of Hræsvelgr.

The name Hræsvelgr is composed of two elements: the words *hræ* and *svelgr*. *Hræ* means a corpse, body or dead creature, and *svelgr* means "the one that swallows".[37] Scholars have therefore, for the most part, explained the name Hræsvelgr as meaning "corpse-swallower" or "body-eater", or simply suggested that the giant lived on the remains of dead animals.[38] Following on from this, certain scholars have even gone so far as to suggest that all giants fed on corpses, the word *jǫtunn* being taken to mean "the one that eats", and the nature of exactly what is eaten being drawn from the interpretation of Hræsvelgr's name.[39]

It might be appropriate to examine this matter a little more closely. For a start, *hræ* does not only mean a "corpse" or "dead animal". It can also mean "flotsam", a "wreck", the "wreckage of a

---

36 *Vafþrúðnismál*, st. 37; *Sæmundar-Edda. Eddukvæði* 1926, 64.
37 Cleasby/Vigfússon 1975.
38 In the *Kulturhistorisk Lexikon*, for example, Halvorsen explains the name Hræsvelgr as meaning "likslukeren" (*KLNM*, 1962), a suggestion echoed in the same year by Lee M. Hollander, who uses the expression "corpse-gulper" (Hollander 1962, 48). More recently, Martin translates the word as "corpse-eater", associating Hræsvelgr with another eagle that appears in *Vǫluspá* (st. 50) and *Skírnismál* (st. 27) (Martin 1981, 359). Machan, in the most recent edition of *Vafþrúðnismál*, finds little to add to this (Machan 1988, 83).
39 von Sydow 1919, 58ff. and references; Halvorsen 1962, 30f.

ship" or the remains of something.[40] The word is used in this sense, for example, in *Landnámabók* where it says, "Austmenn brutu þar skip sitt og gerðu úr hrænum skip þat er þeir kölluðu Trékylli" ("Some Norwegians were shipwrecked ... and from the wreckage of their ship they constructed another that they called Trékylli").[41] Cleasby and Vigfússon also offer the meaning, "scraps or chips of trees or timber". Several examples of this use of the word occur in the thirteenth century lawbook, *Grágás*. In connection with any man whose means of transport gets damaged in another man's wood, *Grágás* states: "þá á hann at höggva til þess sem hann þarf að bæta, ok láta eptir liggja hræ"[42] ("... then he should cut down enough wood to repair it, but leave the remains behind"). Elsewhere in *Grágás*, in relation to damaged boats, we find a similar statement: "eiga þeir at taka við af fjöru manns, ok bæta farkost sinn, ok leggja eptir hræ"[43] ("they should take wood from a man's beach and repair their vessel, and leave the remains behind"). A third example from *Grágás*, regarding tenants, states that "ef hann vill bæta bús-búhluti sína, ok á hann at hafa við til þess, hvárt sem hann vill úr skógi ef fylgir eða af fjöru, ok láta eptir liggja hræ"[44] ("... if he wishes to add to his dwelling, then he should have wood for this purpose, whether it be taken from a wood, should that be attached, or from the shore, but he must leave the remains behind"). This particular meaning is also reflected in the words *hráviði* ("newly cut wood") and *hrár viðr* ("moist wood").

It was mentioned earlier that *svelgr* can mean "swallower" or "gulper". This, however, is not the first interpretation of the word given by Cleasby and Vigfússon. The first meaning of the word in their dictionary is "a swirl, whirlpool or current stream". The examples given for this interpretation are drawn from the *Prose Edda* in connection with the story of *Gróttasǫngr* ("var þar eptir svelgr í hafinu"[45], i.e. "a whirlpool was left in the sea"), and from *Alexanders*

---

40 Cleasby/Vigfússon 1975.
41 ÍF I, 198; *The Book of Settlements*, 1972, 75.
42 Grg Ib, 109.
43 Grg Ib, 124.
44 Grg Ib, 138.
45 *Snorra-Edda* 1935, 177; *Edda* 1987, 107.

saga, which compares a desert sandstorm to a classical whirlpool: "slíkir hascar þickia þar vera á þurru lande sem svelgr i hafe eða Sirtes oc Scylla þeir hascar er sva heita"[46] ("such dangers are said to be on dry land like a whirlpool in the sea, or Sirtes and Scylla as these dangers are called").[47] It is only as a simile that Cleasby and Vigfússon later offer the meaning of "swallower" for *svelgr*. On the other hand, when it comes to the name Hræsvelgr itself, Cleasby and Vigfússon give only a solitary interpretation, i.e. "carrion swallower".

In the light of what has been said about the meaning of the individual words *hræ* and *svelgr*, it seems to me more correct that one should interpret Hræsvelgr as meaning "the one who swallows shipwrecks and other kinds of flotsam adrift on the ocean, and causes them to be sucked down into the depths". This interpretation is much closer to the subject of the strophe in *Vafþrúðnismál* which deals with the sea and sky. Since the question is related to the wind which "ferr vág yfir" ("crosses the sea"), the answer cannot be to do with anything else. It therefore has to be the sea that Hræsvelgr is said to work on in Vafþrúðnir's answer. Naturally, there are all sorts of flotsam and jetsom that get sucked into the depths of the ocean whenever the power in question sends the winds across the surface of the water, creating whirlpools and suction currents that clean up the surface of the ocean. Corpses and dead creatures are not what you would expect to find in the path of the wind in these conditions. It therefore seems obvious to me that the idea of Hræsvelgr being a "corpse-eater" who lives off cadavers and other dead creatures must be based on a misunderstanding.

Hræsvelgr is also mentioned in the *Prose Edda*, and even though his description there is based for the most part on that given in *Vafþrúðnismál*, it is right that it should also be examined here. Snorri writes as follows:

> Þá mælti Gangleri: Hvaðan kemr vindr; hann er sterkr, svá at hann hrærir stór hǫf, ok hann æsir eld; en svá sterkr sem hann er, þá má eigi sjá hann; því er hann undarliga skapaðr. Þá segir Hárr: þat

---

46 *Alexanders saga*, 1925, 50.
47 Regarding the classical reference to Scylla, or Skylla, see *The Odyssey* 1961, 236.

kann ek vel segja þér; á norðanverðum himins enda sitr *jǫtunn* sá, er Hræsvelgr heitir; hann hefir arnarham; en er hann beinir flug, þá standa vindar undar vængjum hans, sem hér segir ...[48]

(Then spoke Gangleri: "Where does the wind come from? It is so strong it stirs great seas and whips up fire, but strong as it is, it cannot be seen. Thus it is marvellously made." Then said High: "I can easily tell you that. At the northernmost end of heaven there sits a giant called Hræsvelgr. He has eagle form. And when he starts to fly winds arise from beneath his wings. It says so here ...")

Following this, Snorri goes on to quote the aforementioned st. 37 of *Vafþrúðnismál*.

Even though Snorri has little to add concerning Hræsvelgr's various characteristics, I feel it right to mention this passage here because Snorri emphasises precisely the point made earlier about the nature of the giant: the wind that he creates "stirs great seas and whips up fire". On the other hand, there is nothing in Snorri's account to support the idea that Hræsvelgr has the habit of eating corpses or the remains of other dead things. Snorri does, however, make one interesting addition regarding Hræsvelgr's domicile. In line with his usual view of the direction in which Jǫtunheimr lies, he states that the giant sits at the northernmost end of the sky, whereas *Vafþrúðnismál* makes no suggestion about which end of the sky Hræsvelgr sits at.

Hræsvelgr is also mentioned amongst the other giants in the name lists provided by the *Prose Edda*. Here, however, nothing is given but the name.[49]

There are no other references to Hræsvelgr in early Scandinavian literature. The conclusion that we draw about him must therefore be based, on the one hand, on what is said about him in the aforementioned works, and on the other, on the meaning of his name. In *Vafþrúðnismál* and the *Prose Edda*, Hræsvelgr is associated with the wind and the sea, and it is most natural, therefore, that one interpret his name in relation to the whirlpools or currents in the ocean that

---

48 *Snorra-Edda* 1935, 40; translation based on *Edda* 1987, 20.
49 *Snorra-Edda* 1935, 245; *Edda* 1987, 155.

swallow and suck down wrecks and other forms of debris that are drifting on the surface of the water.

Of all of those sources which have been preserved from the pre-Christian era and give an uncorrupted picture of the way of thought and world view of the pagan Nordic faith, scaldic poetry is one of the most valuable. Egill Skalla-Grímsson was in his prime in the middle of the ninth century, a time when the Old Norse religion was still in force in Iceland and the other Scandinavian countries. In his individual verses and longer poems, Egill makes a number of references to the giants. *Egils saga* tells, for example, of one occasion when Egill was sailing home from Norway on the open sea: "the wind began to get up and a wind came fresh and favourable. The ship raced along and Egill spoke this verse:

Þél høggr stórt fyr stáli	With its chisel of, the headwind,
stafnkvígs á veg jafnan	scourge of the mast, mightily
út með éla meitli	hones its file by the prow
andærr jǫtunn vandar,	on the path that my sea-bull treads.
en svalbúinn selju	In gusts of wind, that chillful
sverfr eirar vanr þeiri	distroyes of timber planes down
Gestils ǫlpt með gustum	the planks before the head
gandr of stál fyr brandi.[50]	of my sea-king's swan.

Briefly, the verse means the following: the powerful tempest chisels away continuously, creating a smooth sea before the prow of the ship with a rasp of hail; the cold storm files mercilessly at the waves with it (the rasp) before the planks of the prow.[51] The actual meaning of the verse is clear, and there is little disagreement about the main contents. However, what I mean to examine here is what Egill means by the concept "vandar jǫtunn". Nordal and others who have examined this strophe have explained the image on the basis of the word *vǫndr* meaning "mast" and *jǫtunn* meaning "scourge". "The scourge of the mast", then, is the wind which fights against the mast of the ship. Obviously, the poet is talking about the wind blowing across the sea. However, bearing in mind what was pointed

---

50 *ÍF* II, 172; trans. *The Complete Sagas of Icelanders* 1997, I, 114.
51 Sigurður Nordal in *ÍF* II, 1933, 172.

out earlier in connection with *Vafþrúðnismál*, it would seem to be closer to the point if we take this "vandar jǫtunn" who crosses the surface of the sea, and causes the ship to advance, as being none other than Hræsvelgr. In actual fact, there is nothing in the verse that argues against this, and the kenning "vandar jǫtunn" might well be appropriate for the giant who stirs up the winds. The *vǫndr* here would then belong to the *jǫtunn* and be seen as a strong gust of wind which spirals, with a whipping motion, and words like *stormsveipur* ("tornado"), *hvirfilvindur* ("whirlwind") and such like are living examples of how people saw the wind as being a rod- or "whisk"-like phenomenon.

As I mentioned above, the giants make many appearances in Egill's poetry. In *Sonatorrek*, the memorial poem that Egill composed for his son Bǫðvar who drowned off the coast, the poet addresses the *jǫtunn* or god of the sea, Ægir, and his wife, Rán. They have taken Egill's son from him, but he can do nothing against them. (st. 9). In the eight strophe of *Sonatorrek*, Egill calls Ægir "bróðr hroða vágs" (the brother of "Hroði vágs"). "Hroði vágs" is simply the "wave sweeper", the one who cleans all loose objects from the surface of the sea, and destroys them. The term "Hroði vágs" has been interpreted by scholars as meaning "the wind which crosses the sea",[52] but the meaning would be even clearer if one saw "Hroði vágs" as being Hræsvelgr: as mentioned above, the idea behind Hræsvelgr's name implies that he is the one who cleans away whatever is drifting on the surface of the sea, sweeping away all forms of debris that are carried by the current, causing them to be swallowed down below the surface of the water. Hræsvelgr and "Hroði vágs" would therefore seem to be one and the same phenomenon, and either of them might well be termed "the brother of Ægir". Indeed, one might also mention a modern saying in Icelandic which states that "það fari í Hræsvelg sem fer í súginn" (literally, "whatever gets sucked away [goes to waste], goes to Hræsvelgr"). It is of particular interest that the idea of suction and Hræsvelgr should be interchangeable in this connection.

Ægir, the god or giant of the sea, and Hræsvelgr, the god or giant of the wind are not the only *jǫtnar* who represent the elements

---

52 Sigurður Nordal in *ÍF* II, 1933, 249.

in the Old Norse world picture. One can also mention the giant Surtr, who is the representative of fire. Some scholars have also wished to see the fourth element, earth, in the shape of the giant, Gymir, the father of Gerðr who was won over by Freyr.[53] In Old Norse belief, however, Jörðin or Earth was early on connected to Óðinn, who became her husband, and to Þórr, who is known as "Jarðar burr", the son of Earth, and was considered to be their son.

On the basis of what has been discussed above, it seems obvious that the giants were alive and real in the minds of those who respected the Old Norse faith. This is clearly reflected in the most complete poem to have been preserved from the times of the pagan religion, Egill Skalla-Grímsson's *Sonatorrek*. This work gives a good example of a tenth-century man opening up his mind to us, because it is particularly personal. In *Sonatorrek*, Egill often makes direct reference to mythological elements, in fact, approximately thirty times in the space of twenty five strophes. Roughly half of his mythological references are related to the ancient gods, and to Óðinn in particular. The remaining half of the references, however, deal with the giants, or other forces closely connected with them such as the wind and the sea. *Sonatorrek*, therefore, has to be considered a highly valuable source of material on the Nordic gods, giants and men at the time of the Old Norse religion.

Conclusion

On the basis of the above examination, it is possible to make the following brief conclusions:

1. The most reliable sources of information that exist regarding the *jǫtnar* in the Old Norse religion are the mythological poems of the Edda, and scaldic poetry. Snorri Sturluson's *Prose Edda* is an unreliable source concerning the giants and the gods, and the *fornaldarsögur* and Scandinavian folk tales offer an even more corrupted and exaggerated view of them than that found in Snorri's work.

---

53 Olsen 1909, 22. See further Steinsland 1991, 63-65 and works referred to there and Simek 1993, 102 and references.

2. The Nordic gods and giants originally sprang from the same root, and many sources testify to a close family relationship between the giants and certain of the gods. These two families of beings each inhabit in their own territory, but mutual visits seem to have been quite commonplace.

3. In the sources that we have, the giants are known for their wisdom and knowledge of the ancient arts. The gods risk their lives and make great sacrifices in order to share in this wisdom.

4. Numerous stories in the mythological poems of the Edda and other sources describe romantic encounters between the gods and giants. In these matters there seems to be a certain equality between the gods and the giants. The giantesses are just as unprepared to accept the gods as the goddesses are to sleep with the giants.

5. The giants play a large role in the Old Norse cosmology. They are the oldest and the first, and the earth was formed from one of them. As forces of nature, they act the parts of the god/giant of the sea, the god/giant of the wind, the god/giant of fire and (possibly) the god/giant of earth.

Translated by Terry Gunnell

---

*This paper was presented at IAHR's Regional Conference on Circumpolar and Northern Religion in Helsinki, on May 13-18, 1990. It was originally published in *Temenos*, vol. 26. 1990 and there entitled, "Gods and Giants in Old Norse Mythology".

Ágrip

Hræsvelgur í nýju ljósi

Í RITGERÐINNI er gefið yfirlit um guði og jötna í norrænni goðafræði, uppruna þeirra og eðli, skyldleika og margvísleg samskipti. Í inngangi er vikið sérstaklega að helstu flokkum ritaðra heimilda um guði og jötna og þeim skipað í eftirfarandi röð samkvæmt aldri og áreiðanleik: 1. Goðakvæði Sæmundar-Eddu. 2. Dróttkvæði. 3. *Edda* Snorra Sturlusonar. 4. Fornaldarsögur Norðurlanda. 5. Þjóðsögur frá síðari tímum. Gerð er ítarleg grein fyrir heimildargildi hvers flokks fyrir sig samkvæmt nýjustu rannsóknarniðurstöðum. Lögð er sérstök áhersla á að goðakvæðin fornu séu traustari heimildir um jötna en þjóðsögur síðari alda og færð fram rök gegn öndverðum viðhorfum sem fram hafa komið í fræðilegri umræðu.

Rakinn er sameiginlegu uppruni jötna og guða og margvísleg fjölskyldutengsl. Þá er gerð grein fyrir bústöðum hvorra tveggja, Jötunheimi og Ásgarði, legu og landamærum.

Sérstaklega er rakið það sem segir um visku jötna og hve þeir voru geymnir á fornan fróðleik. Dregin eru fram dæmi úr goðakvæðum sem segja frá því hvernig Æsir leituðu til hundvísra jötna, lögðu sig í hættu og kostuðu miklu til, er þeir vildu afla sér lærdóms og fræðslu.

Þá er greint frá brösóttum samskiptum jötna og guða í ástamálum sem birtast í lýsingum á viðbrögðum Freyju við bónorði Þryms og Gerðar við bónorði Freys.

Hlutur jötna í heimsmyndarfræði norrænna trúarbragða er dreginn fram sérstaklega. Er þá fyrst hugað að Hræsvelg, jötninum í arnarham sem samkvæmt *Vafþrúðnismálum* var sagður valdur að vindunum með vængjablaki sínu. Heiti Hræsvelgs hefur lengstaf verið túlkað sem „hrææta", sá sem neytir hræja af dauðum fénaði, dýrum eða mönnum. Í ritgerðinni er sett fram ný skýring á þessu heiti. Vakin er athygli á því að samkvæmt *Grágás* merkti hræ í fornu máli brak úr skipum og svelgur er líklegra til að vera dregið af svelg í hafi en þeim sem gleypir fæðu. Í framhaldi af þessu er Hræsvelgur skýrt sem vindjötunninn/vindguðinn sem veldur rokinu, fer yfir hafið, svelgir og sogar til botns öll hræ og allt brak sem þar kann að fljóta á yfirborði.

Hræsvelgur á sér nokkrar hliðstæður sem jötunn/guð. Er þar fyrstan að nefna bróður hans, Ægi, sævarjötuninn sem einnig hefur stundum til að bera eiginleika sem gera hann goðumlíkan. Aðra hliðstæðu er að finna í

33

eldjötninum Surti sem einnig má sjá sem hvorttveggja í senn, jötun og guð. Þá hefur verið sett fram tilgáta um fjórða jötuninn sem hefði þessa sömu eiginleika, Gymi, föður Gerðar, sem væri þá jarðarjötunn/jarðarguð.

Ef sú tilgáta hefði við nægilega sterk rök að styðjast væri fulltrúa allra höfuðskepnanna að finna í norrænum goðsagnaheimildum um jötna.

Blót *and* Þing.
The Function of the Tenth-Century Goði

I

HÁVAMÁL has the words:

veiztu hvé biðia skal?	Do you know how to petition?
veiztu hvé blóta skal?	Do you know how to sacrifice?
veiztu hvé senda skal?	Do you know how to consign?
veiztu hvé sóa skal? [1]	Do you know how to immolate?

But this source dating from the time of the Old Norse religion is not informative, since the matter at issue is expressed in question form. Yet the next stanza hints at an answer to part of the question, when it says:

Betra er óbeðit	Better unpetitioned
en sé ofblótit,	than extravagant sacrifice,
ey sér til gildis gjǫf;	a gift always looks for a repayment;
betra er ósent	better unconsigned
en sé ofsóit. [2]	than extravagant immolation.

These words display the moderation that marks the ethic of *Hávamál*.[3] On the other hand, we are not much wiser about the real state of religious practice or how cult-observances were performed.

The *Saga of Hákon the Good* contains the following description of the sacrificial ceremonies of Old Norse religion:

Þat var forn siðr, þá er blót skyldi vera, at allir bændr skyldu þar koma, sem hof var, ok flytja þannug fǫng sín, þau er þeir skyldu hafa, meðan veizlan stóð. At veizlu þeiri skyldu allir menn ǫl eiga.

---

1   *Eddadigte* I 1962, 36.
2   Op.cit., 37.
3   Símon Jóh. Ágústsson 1949, 89; 93. Guðmundur Finnbogason 1929, 91. Sigurður Nordal 1942, 199 ff.

Þar var ok drepinn alls konar smali ok svá hross, en blóð þat allt, er þar kom af, þá var kallat hlaut, ok hlautbollar þat, er blóð þat stóð í, ok hlautteinar, þat var svá gǫrt sem støkklar, með því skyldi rjóða stallana ǫllu saman ok svá veggi hofsins útan ok innan ok svá stǫkkva á mennina, en slátr skyldi sjóða til mannfagnaðar. Eldar skyldu vera á miðju gólfi í hofinu ok þar katlar yfir. Skyldi full um eld bera, en sá, er gerði veizluna ok hǫfðingi var, þá skyldi hann signa fullit ok allan blótmatinn, skyldi fyrst Óðins full – skyldi þat drekka til sigrs ok ríkis konungi sínum – en síðan Njarðar full ok Freys full til árs ok friðar. Þá var mǫrgum mǫnnum títt að drekka þar næst bragafull. Menn drukku ok full frænda sinna, þeira er heygðir höfðu verit, ok váru þat minni kǫlluð.[4]

(It was ancient custom, when there was to be a *blót*, that all the householders should come to where the *hof* was, and bring their supplies there, those they were to use while the feast lasted. At that feast everybody should share the ale. All kinds of animals were slaughtered, including horses, and all the blood that ran from them was called *hlaut*, and *hlaut*-bowels what the blood stood in, and there were *hlaut*-twigs – made like aspergilla – with them all the stalls and the walls of the *hof* outside and in should be blooded and the men sprinkled as well, and the meat should be boiled to make them good cheer. There should be fires in the middle of the floor of the *hof* and cauldrons over them. Drinks were to be passed over the fire, and the man who made the feast and was the leader should "sign" the drink and all the *blót*-food: first Óðinn's toast – that should be drunk for victory and the might of their king, and then Njörðr's toast and Freyr's for a good season and freedom from strife. Then it was many men's custom to drink next the *bragafull*. Men also drank toasts to their kinsmen, those who had been mound-buried, and they were called "memorials").

The description of an ancient sacrificial ceremony by Snorri Sturluson has no complete analogue in Old Norse texts, and scholars have debated whether Snorri composed the account himself or relied on an older text. Bjarni Aðalbjarnarson in his edition of *Heimskringla* in 1941 considered this chapter as Snorri's original work.[5] In *Eyrbyggja saga* there is a description of the cult-centre of Þórólfr Mostrarskegg, in which the following passage has some resemblance to Snorri's description:

4   ÍF XXVI 1941, 167-168.
5   Bjarni Aðalbjarnarson, op. cit.,lxxxviii.

Á stallanum skyldi ok standa hlautbolli, ok þar í hlautteinn sem
støkkull væri, ok skyldi þar støkkva með ór bollanum blóði því, er
hlaut var kallat; þat var þess konar blóð, er svæfð váru þau kvik-
endi, er goðunum var fórnat.[6]

(A *hlaut*-bowl should also stand on the stall, and in it a hlaut-twig,
as if it were an aspergillum, and with that the blood that was
called *hlaut* should be sprinkled from the bowl; blood it was of
that kind {which ran} when the animals were despatched which
were offered to the gods).

Eyrbyggja was written in the thirteenth century, but scholars are
not agreed as to how early in the century. When Einar Ól. Sveinsson
edited *Eyrbyggja* in *Íslenzk fornrit*, he dated the saga to about 1220.[7]
On the other hand, Sigurður Nordal, in his essay of 1953 in *Nordisk
kultur*, judged that *Eyrbyggja* was written about 1250,[8] and various
scholars have accepted his view.[9] The dating of the saga is relevant
to the chapter under discussion and to a conceivable textual relation
between *Eyrbyggja* and *Heimskringla* which is dated about 1230.[10]
When the wording of the text in each source is compared, the probability becomes striking. Finnur Jónsson compared the two passages
in 1898, and wrote: "the best indication that this is one and the
same account is the fact that in both passages the sacrificial twig is
compared to an aspergillum; it is improbable, not to say impossible,
that the same idea would have occurred to two different authors."[11]
Finnur judged that Snorri was the first to compose this passage, and
that it reached *Eyrbyggja* from him. Finnur came to this conclusion
even though he dated *Eyrbyggja* before *Heimskringla*; he made it
square with this dating by regarding the passage as an interpolation
in *Eyrbyggja*.[12] Einar Ól. Sveinsson has evident difficulty in explain-
ing the relation between these two passages, and he says: "For my
part, I think it likely that the passage in *Eyrbyggja* is based on a
memorandum by Ari or one of his school (I see no reason to regard

6   *ÍF* IV 1935, 8ff.
7   Einar Ól. Sveinsson, op.cit., xiii. See further, by the same author, *Scripta Islandica* 1968,
    3-18.
8   Sigurður Nordal in *Nordisk kultur* VIII B 1953, 248.
9   See Jakob Benediktsson in *ÍF* I, lxiv, note 26 and the works referred to there.
10 Bjarni Aðalbjarnarson in *ÍF* XXVI, xxix. Sigurður Nordal in *NK* VIII B, 219
11 Finnur Jónsson 1898, 30.
12 Ibid.

it as an interpolation, for it has the same stamp as much else in the saga), but I am not prepared to decide whether Snorri is following this very document or *Eyrbyggja* itself." [13]

It has been suggested that there is no need to postulate a written source for these two texts, since to a Catholic it would seem a matter of course to represent the sacrificial twig as an aspergillum, in order to give the reader an idea of its use. [14] Yet this interpretation does not seem to me quite satisfactory, because even though there is a superficial similarity between sprinkling blood and sprinkling holy water, the ceremonies in question are of totally different nature. Holy water was sprinkled as a symbol of purification, but blood was sprinkled to charge the surroundings with power, as will appear later. Of course, the difference in kind need not have stopped a Christian author from seizing on the parallel of the aspergillum when he had to represent the sacrificial twig of ancient worship, but it seems to me more doubtful whether Christian writers of the thirteenth or fourteenth centuries were in general aware of how the twig was used. So I judge it right to assume textual contact between the two sources here in question.

Considering that there are strong arguments for placing *Eyrbyggja* some twenty years later than *Heimskringla*, it is natural to suppose that the author of *Eyrbyggja* was drawing on Snorri when he wrote this passage. But before clinching the matter it is as well to look at some particular points.

Snorri's account of the sacrificial ceremony is fuller and more detailed. He says, for instance, that the blood was sprinkled on the people, whereas *Eyrbyggja* states simply that blood was sprinkled, without specifying how or where. If both writers were following a memorandum by Ari, it could be supposed either that Snorri added "people" or that the author of *Eyrbyggja* omitted the point. As far as Ari is concerned (or one of his school), he was hardly likely to go into detail about ancient worship. In a different connection, I have had occasion to examine Ari's handling of Old Norse religious ceremony, and there he seems to make every effort to go as far as a conscientious historian possibly could not to give a close description

13 Einar Ól. Sveinsson in *ÍF* IV, xiv.
14 Jóhannes Halldórsson in *ÍF* XIV, viii ff.

38

of events.[15] It is also proper to remember that Ari held office within the Church in close association with bishops, which must have affected the subjects he undertook and his treatment of them. So I think, in the light of what we know of Ari and his methods, that it is advisable to abandon the hypothesis that he (or someone of his unspecified school) was the originator of the account of sprinkling people with blood at Old Norse sacrifices in a cult-centre. This conclusion reinforces the view that the whole description of the sacrifice originated in Snorri's work; so we must now look at his data.

Snorri was some 100 years younger than Ari the Wise (he was born in 1178/9). From early youth he must have had an unusually good education by the standards of the time, and his attitude to religion was altogether different from Ari's. Snorri was a young man when the Archbishop wrote to Iceland forbidding the ordination of chieftains; so he was early obliged to choose between lay and clerical office, and he became a secular magnate, never taking office in the Church.[16] At the peak of his career (1218-20), Snorri travelled to Norway and Sweden. There he immersed himself in poetry, and as a result applied himself especially to the study of Old Norse mythology, and seems to have collected all the material he could possibly lay hands on. From both *Heimskringla* and *Snorra Edda* it is clear that his aim was to collect and publish information on Old Norse religion.[17] The description of the sacrificial feast at Hlaðir fits well into this framework. Snorri may have received this account of procedure from other tales of Sigurður Hlaðajarl, but we are not compelled to believe that he did. Perhaps it is just as likely that he was able to get hold of a description of ancient sacrificial rites in Sweden, since the heathen religion there was flourishing in some places as late as about 1200,[18] that is, a short time before Snorri was in the area. Thus, Old Norse religious rites were chronologically nearer to Snorri while he was investigating these matters in Norway

---

15 Jón Hnefill Aðalsteinsson 1978, 130 ff.

16 *Sturlunga saga* I 1946, 271 ff. *DI* I 1857-76, 291. Helgi Þorláksson in *Snorri, átta alda minning* 1979, 70 ff.

17 Óskar Halldórsson in *Snorri, átta alda minning* 1979, 94 ff. and works referred to there. There is probably a little too much emphasis here on Snorri's interest in collecting all that he could find about the Old Norse religion. See further below, on p. 76.

18 Ljungberg 1938, 281 ff.

and Sweden than they were to Ari in Iceland 100 years earlier. And Snorri's attitude to this material was totally unlike Ari's.

Therefore I think that everything points to Snorri as the original author of the *Heimskringla* passage on the sacrifice at Hlaðir, and that the author of *Eyrbyggja* drew on Snorri when he was compiling the saga.[19]

Finally we have to consider the actual gist of the passage, and how likely it is that Snorri based his accoumt on genuine traditions. Anne Holtsmark doubted whether Snorri was right in assuming that blood was sprinkled on the congregation. Probably it was simply splashed or daubed on the images of the gods.[20] But against this is the testimony that in some religions, Mithraism for instance, blood was sprinkled in much the same way as Snorri describes.[21] Reference may also be made to the episode of blood-offerings to ghosts in the *Odyssey*, where the spirits of the dead are revived and can communicate once blood is administered to them.[22] And the feast at Hlaðir was intended for the spirits of the departed no less than the gods, as appears in the citation just made. Gabriel Turville-Petre has well interpreted Snorri's idea of the sacrificial feast, and I quote his words: "The meaning of the sacrificial feast, as Snorri saw it, is fairly plain. When blood was sprinkled over altars and men and the toasts were drunk, men were symbolically joined with gods of war and fertility, and with their dead ancestors, sharing their mystical powers. This is a form of communion."[23]

So I think it reasonable to suppose that Snorri bases his description on sound traditions. Some elements were assimilated in Christian usage, such as the toast, and the sharing of food. Snorri's term, *hlaut*, that is, the blood of the sacrifice, has caused scholars some trouble. It is related to the verb *að hljóta*, and is current in Old Norse texts, for instance in *Hymiskviða*, where it is said that the gods "hristo teina / ok á hlaut sá"[24] (shook twigs and surveyed the *hlaut*),

19 In *Kjalnesinga saga,* ÍF XIV, 7 there is a description of a *hof* based on *Eyrbyggja, Heim-skringla* and other sources. See Jóhannes Halldórsson in ÍF XIV, xi.

20 Holtsmark in *ANF* 64 1949, 47.

21 Cumont 1956, 162; 180ff. See further Jón Hnefill Aðalsteinsson 1997a, 207-217.

22 The *Odyssey* of Homer 1903, 176-177.

23 Turville-Petre 1964, 251. See further Dillmann 1997, 65-69.

24 *Eddadigte* II 1965, 40.

and *Vǫluspá* mentions selecting *hlaut*-twigs[25] ("kjósa hlautvið"). The connection between the Eddic poems and Snorri is not clear, but I think it most natural to interpret Snorri's *hlaut* as some item in the process of divination which was certainly part of the sacrificial ceremonies of Old Norse religion.[26] The terms *að ganga til fréttar*[27] (to enquire about the future) and *gá blótsins*[28] (scrutinise the offerings) were both used of this practice.

II

In some Old Norse texts the times of sacrifice are mentioned. Snorri says in *Heimskringla*: "Þá skyldi blóta í móti vetri til árs, en at miðjum vetri blóta til gróðrar, it þriðja at sumri, þat var sigurblót".[29] (Towards winter, sacrifice should be made for a good season, and at midwinter for good growth: the third, when summer came, that was a victory-*blót*). What Snorri says about three principal sacrifices annually is supported by various independent texts. Some passages in the Family Sagas mention an autumn sacrifice shortly before the Winter Nights. In *Gísla saga Súrssonar* we find: "Þorgrímr ætlaði at hafa haustboð at vetrnóttum ok fagna vetri ok blóta Frey..."[30] (Þorgrímr intended to have an autumn feast at the time of the Winter Nights to welcome winter and sacrifice to Freyr). The term *Þorrablót*[31] is good evidence of a midwinter sacrifice; and in *Vatnsdæla saga* there is an illusion to sacrifice in the first days of summer:

> Nú mun Ljót, móðir hans, blóta í mót sumri, sem hún er vǫn at þeira sið...[32]

25 *Eddadigte* I 1962, 14.
26 In *Vǫluspá* 1952, 147, Sigurður Nordal interprets the lines just quoted from *Hym.* as follows: "They sprinkled the blood of sacrifice, and interpreted the bloodmarks on the sacrificial chips". See further Jón Hnefill Aðalsteinsson 1978, 51; 1997a, 189-195 and works referred to there.
27 Meissner 1917, 18 ff.
28 Jón Hnefill Aðalsteinsson 1978, 18 ff. and the works referred to there.
29 *ÍF* XXVI 1941, 20.
30 *ÍF* VI 1943, 50.
31 In *KLNM* XX 1976, 395-397, E. F. Halvorsen judges that it is not inappropriate to interpret *þorrablót* as a sacrifice conducted in the month Þorri. See further Holtsmark in *KLNM* V 1960, 366-368; also *ÍF* XXVI 1941, 63.
32 *ÍF* VIII; 67.

(Now his mother, Ljót, will sacrifice towards summer, as she usually does according to their religion...).

The inference to be drawn from these sources is that most probably Old Norse religion had three chief sacrifices, at the times of the Winter Nights, near midwinter and at the approach of summer. Sacrifices were in fact probably far more frequent, but the others would evidently have been minor ceremonies or else sacrifices for a particular purpose.

The timing of the chief sacrifices is of some importance when we consider the connection between sacrifices and assemblies; that is, between secular business and ritual, and hence the part of the *goðar* played in each of these areas. Assemblies in Iceland were held at specific times, as *Grágás* prescribes: "skapþing III: vorþing, alþingi oc leið"[33] (three established assemblies; the spring meeting, the General Assembly and the autumn meeting). Spring assemblies were held after the fourth week of summer, and were to be held between the end of May and the sixth week of summer. Thus spring assemblies could be held from about 7 May up to 27 May according to our calendar. The General Assembly began on the Thursday of the eleventh week of summer (Thor's day), and a week earlier before A.D. 1000. Finally the autumn assembly was held after the General Assembly. It fell at the earliest 14 days after the General Assembly (1 July) and at the latest at the end of August.[34]

If the occasions of the chief sacrificial feasts were as argued above, they will have taken place apart from the times when assemblies were held. Considering distances and communications in tenth-century Iceland, it is obvious that conditions of transit were quite different between the different times for sacrifices and for assemblies. Many routes used in summer were impossible in winters, especially mountain-tracks; but conversely winter frosts could bridge large rivers and make neighbours of those who had difficulty in reaching each other in the summer. So it is not to be expected that the cult-centres for sacrifices should be located where assemblies were held.

I draw attention to this matter because last century the theory was put forward that the power of the *goðar* in Icelandic assemblies

33 *Grágás* Ia, 140. *Grágás* II, 277.
34. *Grágás* Ia, 94 and passim. Cf. Jón Jóhannesson 1956, 64; 101-102.

derived from the chieftains of the land-taking who initially set up cult-centres, and enacted sacrifices on their own behalf and for those settlers who had not the resources to found cult-centres for themselves. These religious gatherings at cult-centres were supposed to have changed gradually into meetings of an administrative kind, and thus the institution of assemblies and the function of the *goðar* sprang from the worship of the gods.[35] It is as well to keep in mind that the scholars who proposed this theory, Konrad Maurer for instance, took the view that the religious office and secular administration were equally important aspects of the functions of the *goðar* in the tenth century.[36]

The scholar who has in this century written most about the early constitution of Iceland and the position of the *goðar* in particular, is Ólafur Lárusson. He made a detailed investigation of the matter in question in the article "Hof and þing", which he published some 50 years ago.[37]

Ólafur Lárusson addressed himself to a study of the distances between the assembly-sites of the Quarters and the names of cult-sites in each Quarter on the one hand, and on the other hand the distances between assembly-sites and the homes of ancestral founders of chieftainly families. The result of the investigation showed that there was by and large a considerable distance between assembly-sites and sites having the element *hof*: from 4 to 20 km as the crow flies. Likewise there was quite a distance between the homes of the founding fathers and the assembly-sites.[38]

Ólafur sums up thus:

> Rannsókn á sambandinu milli hofa og þinga virðist mér bera þess ljósan vott, að frá upphafi hafi ekki verið um neitt náið samband þeirra að ræða, og þessi niðurstaða er veigamikil röksemd gegn þeirri almennu skoðun, að stjórnarskipun Íslands hafi verið af trúarlegum rótum runnin.[39]
>
> (Investigation of the correspondence between cult-centres and assembly sites seems to me to show clearly that from the start

---

35 Maurer 1852, 59 ff.
36 Op. cit., 82 ff: 111 ff.
37 Ólafur Lárusson 1958, 91-99.
38 Op. cit., 92-98.
39 Op. cit., 99.

there was no close connection, and this result is a significant argument against the general opinion that the constitution of Iceland sprang from religious origins.)

I have thought it right to recapitulate these chief points because of the great influence of Ólafur Lárusson's article and the way it has shaped scholars' attitudes to this matter.

Some fifty years after this article was written, things have taken on a rather different aspect. First, the place-name element of *hof* is no longer used as a point of reference in the same way. There is still much uncertainty about cult-centres in Iceland; although it seems probable that tenth-century Icelanders had "samkomustaði til trúariðkana og nefnt þá hof" (meeting places for the practice of religion called *hof*) as Kristján Eldjárn put it,[40] too little is as yet known on this subject to warrant the conclusions that Ólafur Lárusson drew. The names of cult-centres and other evidence such as ruins and artefacts remain to a great extent unexplored to this day.[41]

Furthermore, Ólafur does not allow for the probability that sacrifices and assemblies were held at different times. If it is true, as I have argued, that the principal sacrifices were conducted during the winter, whereas assemblies were convened in the summer season, it is not to be expected that the same centres were used for the two different gatherings. From this point of view, Ólafur Lárusson's article has no particular authority, and is not a convincing argument for the association of assembly and sacrifice under Old Norse heathendom. This aspect of the article has been much overrated during the last fifty years.[42]

III

Two passages in Old Icelandic texts refer expressly to the function of the *goði* in the tenth century. The first is in the chapter of *Eyrbyggja saga* already cited on the cult-centre of Þórólfr Mostrarskegg, where the description runs as follows:

40 Kristján Eldjárn 1974, 111.
41 Op. cit., 111-112.
42 Ólafur Lárusson in *KLNM* V 1960, 363-366 and works referred to there. See further Björn Þorsteinsson 1966, 89.

Innar af hofinu var hús í þá líking, sem nú er sǫnghús í kirkjum, ok stóð þar stalli á miðju gólfinu sem altari, ok lá þar á hringr einn mótlauss, tvítøgeyringr, ok skyldi þar at sverja eiða alla; Þann hring skyldi hofgoði hafa á hendi sér til allra mannfunda... Umhverfis stallann var goðunum skipat í afhúsinu. Til hofsins skyldu allir menn tolla gjalda ok vera skyldir hofgoðanum til allra ferða, sem nú eru þingmenn hǫfðingjum, en goði skyldi hofi uppi halda af sjálfs síns kostnaði, svá at eigi rénaði, ok hafa inni blótveizlur.[43]

(In the inner part of the hof was a room in a form similar to the chancel of churches nowadays; and a stall stood in the middle of the floor there, like an altar, on which lay a twenty-ounce pennanular ring, and all oaths should be sworn on it. The hofgoði should wear that ring on his arm at all public meetings... In the room (the images of) the gods were disposed around the stall. All men should pay tolls to the hof, and be bound to follow the hofgoði on all journeys, as þingmenn are now bound to follow their leaders, but the goði should maintain the hof at his own expense, so that it did not deteriorate, and hold blót-feasts in it.)

In *Landnámabók (Hauksbók)* and other Old Icelandic texts a legal section is incorporated, which has been called Úlfljótr's Laws. I give here an extract from *Landnámabók*:

Baugr tvíeyringr eða meiri skyldi liggja í hverju hǫfuðhofi á stalla; þann baug skyldi hverr goði hafa á hendi sér til lǫgþinga allra, þeira er hann skyldi sjálfr heyja, ok rjóða hann þar áðr í roðru nautsblóðs þess, er hann blótaði þar sjálfr. Hverr sá maðr, er þar þurfti lǫgskil af hendi at leysa at dómi, skyldi áðr eið vinna at þeim baugi ...[44]

(A ring of two ounces or more should be on the stall in each principal *hof*; each *goði* should wear that ring on his arm at all established assemblies in which he himself should participate, and redden it beforehand in gore from the blood of the beast he personally sacrificed there. Everyone who needed to perform legal duties there at court should previously swear an oath on that ring.)

---

43 *ÍF* IV 1935, 8-9.
44 *ÍF* I 1968, 313; 315. Cf. Foote 1974, 69-86, and Jón Hnefill Aðalsteinsson 1978, 34 ff. and works referred to there.

We need to look more closely at these texts and distinguish separate elements and particular points in them.

Eyrbyggja saga

1. The cult centre is described with reference to a church.
2. The pedestall or stall is compared to an altar.
3. A ring without join to the value of 20 ounces.
4. The *goði* of the cult-centre was to wear the ring on his arm at all meetings.
5. All oaths to be sworn on the ring. (This is stated before it is said that the *hofgoði* must wear the ring on his arm at all meetings. This form of wording might suggest that the author imagined that oaths were sworn within the cult-centre).

Landnámabók

1. The term "chief cult centre" implies other cult-centres.
2. There is no comment on the pedestall.
3. A ring to the value of two ounces, ca. 54 grams.[45]
4. Each *goði* was to wear the ring on his arm at all meetings he took part in. Before holding court, he must redden the ring in the blood of the beast that the *goði* himself sacrificed at the assembly.
5. Every man who had legal duties to perform at court in the assembly must first take an oath on this ring.

In *Hávamál* it says: "Baugeið Óðinn / hygg ek at unnit hafi"[46] (I think that Óðinn took an oath on the ring), and in *Atlakviða*, Atli is said to have taken at oath "at hringi Ullar"[47] (on the ring of Ullr). In the *Anglo-Saxon Chronicle* we hear of a Viking army which confirmed a truce with king Alfred in 878 by an oath: "on þam halgan beage"[48] (on the holy ring). In the light of these sources, scholars are agreed that oaths were sworn on a ring in the period of Old Norse heathendom. But recollection of this practice had faded in Iceland in the thirteenth century, as can be seen from the text of *Eyrbyggja*, where it is not clear whether the oath was sworn within the cult-centre or at the general assembly. In this connection we may recall the account in *Víga-Glúms saga* of Víga-Glúmr's oath, which he is said to have sworn at cult-centres.[49]

---

45 Magnús Már Lárusson 1958, 243. Jón Jóhannesson 1956, 390-398.
46 *Eddadigte* I 1962, 30.
47 *Edda. Die Lieder des Codex Regius* 1962, 245.
48 Plummer 1892-99 s. a. 876. See further, *The Anglo-Saxon Chronicle* 1953 (1978), 74-75.
49 *ÍF* IX 1956, 85 f.

When the passages from *Eyrbyggja* and Úlfljótr's Laws are compared, it is the difference in precision between these two texts that immediately strikes the eye. The author of *Eyrbyggja* speaks of "all the oaths" without specifying their purpose or their location, whereas the author of Úlfljótr's Laws states exactly, when and where oaths must be sworn, and for what purpose. The author of *Eyrbyggja* speaks of "general meetings" without further definition, whereas the author of Úlfljótr's Laws specifies a court held by the *goði* in question. The author of *Eyrbyggja* refers twice to a church in order to describe the cult-centre, and at the close of the passage he alludes once more to contemporary conditions by mentioning assembly-men and chieftains. By contrast, the author of the passage in Úlfljótr's Laws nowhere refers to contemporary conditions or other matters outside the text, except in so far as the concept "chief cult-centre" implies other centres. So the fundamental difference between these two passages is clear. The extract from *Eyrbyggja* bears the marks of an author describing objects and events with which he is not familiar but has heard of from more or less indistinct traditions. This is actually to be expected, when we are dealing with a thirteenth-century author who tries to describe objects, events and circumstances current 250 years earlier.

The text of Úlfljótr's Laws is a different matter altogether. There the exactitude characteristic of Icelandic legal texts prevails, and the author takes the utmost pains to phrase his definitions so clearly and explicitly as to exclude all doubt about the sense. The terms *þar* (there), *áðr* (before) and *sjálfr* (himself) are all repeated so as to avoid any misunderstanding, either about the part taken by the *goði* or by those who had to swear an oath on the ring.

I am here concerned to discover on the one hand the reason for the divergence of these two texts and on the other hand where the author of Úlfljótr's Laws got his information about the proceedings of the *goði* at the assembly. In seeking a model for this text, it is natural to think first of the legal texts surviving in *Grágás*. There is an allusion to sacrifice in the article on: "blóta eigi heiðnar vættir"[50] (not sacrificing to heathen spirits). There, all are lumped together, the gods of ancient religion and such other beings as men might

---

50 *Grágás* Ia, 22. *Grágás* II, 27.

conceivably appeal to. The idea apparent in this decree is that belief in the old gods is to be classed with all other superstition and idol-worship that might be concerned. Elsewhere in *Grágás* there is another allusion to sacrifice where passages from the texts of truce-agreements and peace guarantees are given; it is laid down in so many words that a decree is to be in force as far as: "Kristnir menn kirkjur sækja, heiðnir menn hof blóta"[51] (Christians attend churches, heathens sacrifice at cult-centres). In these set formulas, which are also found in other works,[52] sacrifice is associated with the cult-centre as firmly and naturally as Christianity with churches. Therefore the author of Úlfljótr's Laws could not have taken his example of the *goði* performing sacrifice at the assembly from surviving texts of *Grágás* which make specific reference to sacrifice.

In *Grágás* there are directions for normal inauguration of the assembly by *goðar*, stating:

> Goðar þeir allir er í því þingi ero. scolo coma til þings ondverðz. Goði sa er þing hælgi a þar hann scal hælga enn fyrsta aptan er þeir coma til þings[53]... En Leið scal sva hælga iamt sem þing.[54]

> (All the chieftains who belong to the assembly are to come to the beginning of the assembly. The chieftain who has the duty of formal inauguration there is to inaugurate the assembly on the first evening they come to the assembly... An autumn meeting is to be formally inaugurated just like an assembly).

These directions are probably a survival of the function fulfilled by the *goði* at the assembly before the Conversion, a matter I shall consider later. It is not known now what procedure the *goði* followed in inaugurating the assembly under Christianity, but of course there was no sacrifice in the ceremony after the year 1000, when public sacrifice was made illegal.[55] But it is reasonable to suppose that sections of truce- and peace-agreements were recited. Thus there was no good reason to infer sacrifice by the *goði* at the assembly from his

---

51 *Grágás* Ia, 205 ff.
52 *ÍF* III 1934, 312. *ÍF* VII 1936, 232-233. *Opuscula*, Vol. I 1960, 164-165.
53 *Grágás* Ia, 97.
54 *Grágás* Ia, 112.
55 *ÍF* I 1968, 17.

inaugural rites under Christianity, let alone describe in detail a procedure which had not been practised for some 200 years.

The verb *blóta* "to sacrifice" is common in various texts of the twelfth and thirteenth centuries. I have looked up some 160 instances in the *Dictionary of the Arnamagnæan Institute in Copenhagen*, to try and discover whether there exists any prototype or parallel for the usage in Úlfljótr's Laws. I have also turned up many of these examples in context. The principal feature of all of them is their vagueness about sacrifice; thus it is not always clear who were the recipients of sacrifice, whether they were heathen gods or something else. It appears however that about 100 instances are sacrifices to heathen gods, heathen spirits or idols. There are eight cases where there is reference to sacrificing to the dead, and another eight where there is reference to sacrifice to devils or underworld deities; there are seven cases where the subject is sacrifice to external nature. In some cases, sacrificial ceremonies have turned into sorcery, and in 16 instances the verb *blóta* has come to signify cursing or imprecation. 14 references concern sacrifice to animals, and often it is specified how they are processed and bewitched through sacrifice. Barely 20 examples refer to the site, and in 14 of these it is a cult-centre. Only twice is there reference to a sacrifice which could have taken place in the vicinity of an assembly.[56]

Nowhere in these texts from the *Dictionary* are there any examples that could serve as parallels to or prototypes of the passage in Úlfljótr's Laws.

The main conclusions that I draw from my investigation are as follows:

1. A comparison of the passage in Úlfljótr's Laws and the corresponding one in *Eyrbyggja* reveals the latter as a prime example of half-forgotten traditions, whereas the former is of totally different cast, written with confidence and authority.
2. The minute and close description in Úlfljótr's Laws of how the *goði* performed sacrifice at the assembly is without parallel in narratives of sacrificial ceremonies.
3. The passage in Úlfljótr's Laws is typical of concise, carefully-

---

56 *The Dictionary of the Arnamagnean Institute in Copenhagen: blóta.*

phrased legal terminology. The content is quite foreign to *Grágás*, where sacrifice is associated with a cult-centre and with heathen spirits.

All in all, I think the most plausible way of accounting for this passage is that we have here an ancient fossilised legal text which goes back to the tenth century.[57]

If this is indeed the remnant of a text old enough to attest the procedure of the *goðar* at the assembly before the Conversion, then we have evidence of their two-fold function and the close link between what was later called spiritual and secular authority. But we should remember that no such dualism existed in the minds of the *goðar*; rather, their situation was all of a piece, the one function sustaining the other. The religious ceremony of sacrifice was probably as natural an element in their duties at the assembly as the other functions later designated as secular.

IV

A certain point of view has often cropped up in discussion of the duties of the tenth century *goðar*, especially on the subject of whether their duties were primarily religious or social. According to this view, it is very unlikely that the power of the *goðar* outlived the Conversion, if the main function of the *goðar* was of a religious kind.[58] In scholarly work, this position is often unsupported by argument, but it seems to be regarded as somehow self-evident that priests of the older faith must have faded away at the Conversion and that priests of the new faith took over. That is indeed what often happens when there is a change of faith.

The Conversion of Iceland did not proceed by any such general rule, but on the contrary in highly unusual circumstances. Many factors in combination contributed to making the Conversion of Ice-

---

57 In *The Conversion of Iceland* 1975, 41, Dag Strömbäck holds a similar opinion where this passage of Úlfljótr's Laws is concerned. He writes: "This passage from the ancient law has an authentic flavour, and there is no reason to suppose that it is the invention of some meddling editor of the thirteeneth century." Cf. note 1. See further Olaf Olsen 1966, 48 ff. where he expresses the view that Úlfljótr's Laws are a thirteenth century invention.

58 Ólafur Lárusson in *KLNM* V 1960, 364. Jakob Benediktsson 1974, 173.

land what it was. One element was the social and political aspect manifested in the attempts of the *goðar* to retain their power.[59] Another was the religious aspect, involved in the decision of the heathen *goðar* to change their faith. They changed religions on the basis of a wise decision reached by well-tried methods acceptable to their faith and their outlook.[60] Thus they shifted their religious alignment, but apparently changed little else in their life or conduct. And, however remarkable it may seem, the *goðar* retained some of their religious functions after the Conversion. Now we see a *goði* raising the symbol of Christianity, the cross, and addressing God Almighty, in a passage in *Grágás* where a *goði* "led into the law" a slave who had been freed:

> Hann scal i lög leiða Goðe sa er hann er iþingi með. Hann scal taca cross ihönd ser, oc nefna vatta Jþat vætte, at hann vinnr eið at crossi lög eið. oc segi ec þat Gvðe, at hann mvn hallda lögom sem sa maðr er vel heldr, oc hann vill þa vera ilögom með oðrom monnom, þeim se goþ gramt er þvi nitir nema fe sino bøte.[61]

> (The chieftain to whose assembly he belongs is to lead him into the law. He is to take a cross in his hand and name witnesses to witness that he swears an oath on the cross, a lawful oath, and "I say before God" that he will keep the laws like a man who keeps them well, and it is his wish then to share in the laws with other men. "God be harsh on him who denies him that unless he atones for it with his goods.")

Attention must be drawn to the end of the *Grágás* formula in *Konungsbók*, especially the words "Goð gramt". Cleasby and Vigfússon supposed that this formula was originally heathen, and read in full: "Mér sé goð holl ef ek satt segi, gröm ef ek lyg."[62] (May the

---

59 Strömbäck 1975, 34-37; Sigurður Líndal 1974, 243 ff.; Björn M. Ólsen 1900, 102 ff.; and Lindow 1979, 179.

60 Jón Hnefill Aðalsteinsson 1978, 124 ff. Foote 1979 (1982), 155-159. Lindow, op. cit., 178-179.

61 *Grágás* Ia, 192. The quotation is taken from the *Konungsbók* manuscript of *Grágás*. In the *Staðarhólsbók* manuscript the wording is: "...þeim er Guð gramr er því nítir nema fe sino böti" (God is harsh on him who denies him that unless he atones for it with his goods.) In the latter a prayer concerning a legal ritual has become a direct statement.

62 Cleasby and Guðbrandur Vigfússon 1874, 211.

gods be favourable if I tell the truth, offended if I lie). But "goð gramt" is not a normal heathen expression – since the gods are addressed in the plural for preference – nor is it a normal form of address to the Christian God, who is well known to be masculine. But for a while in the first years of Christianity Christ was called *goð*. This appears for instance in Steinunn's stanza, "Lítt hykk goð gætti", meaning that Christ was not able to protect the ship of the missionary Þangbrandr.[63] The date of *Grágás* formula has been placed at the same time as the stanza, or a little later.[64] If this is right, the formula gives evidence of the *goðar* entering straight into a religious function under Christianity, turning to the Christian God without any intermediary.

In the early years of Icelandic Christianity, the only bishops in the country were peripatetic, and priests were rare.[65] Information about this period is very scanty, but there are pieces of evidence which enable us to estimate the position of the *goðar* as against the new priesthood.

One of the oldest surviving documents on this period is the *Ævi Snorra goða* (The Life of Snorri Goði), who was barely forty when Christianity was made law and who survived the first three decades of Christianity. Snorri's daughter, Þuríðr, was one of Ari's informants, so it was a short step from Snorri to the first work of history.[66] The life of Snorri occupies only two pages, which record no more than the main events of his life and the name of his children, nineteen freeborn and three by slaves.[67] Snorri lived at two farms, Helgafell and Tunga, after the introduction of Christianity. It is said of him:

> Hann lét kirkju gera at Helgafelli, en aðra í Tungu í Sælingsdal; en sumir segja, at hann léti gera í annat sinn at Helgafelli með Guðrúnu kirkju, þá er sú brann, er hann hafði gera látit... var Snorri goði grafinn heima þar í Sælingsdalstungu at þeiri kirkju, er hann sjálfr hafði gera látit.[68]

63 Finnur Jónsson 1908-15, B1, 128; A1, 136.
64 Baetke 1973, 141.
65 Sigurður Nordal 1942, 285 ff. and Sigurður Líndal 1974, 249 ff.
66 *ÍF* I 1968, 4.
67 *ÍF* IV 1935, 166.
68 Ibid.

(He had a church built at Helgafell and another at Tunga in Sæ-
lingsdalur; and some people say that he, together with Guðrún,
had a church built all over again at Helgafell when the one he had
made there burnt down... Snorri was buried at home there, at the
church at Sælingsdalstunga which he himself had built).

The text is reliable evidence that from the first days of Christianity[69] the *goðar had* been responsible for religious worship, and
founded churches. If the record of Snorri's first foundation at Helgafell is correct, that church was built during the first decade of
Christianity. Yet the *goði* could not discharge the priestly office, and
therefore as patron of a church he would have had to educate a
priest. *Grágás* says on this point:

Þat er manne rétt, at lata læra prestling, til kirkju sinnar, hann scal
gera maldaga við sveininn sjálfan. ef hann er .xvi. vetra, enn ef
hann er yngri. þa scal hann gera við lograþanda hans. Sa maldagi a
at haldaz allr. er þeir gera með ser... Ef prestr flér kirkio þa er hann
er til lærþr. eþa firriz sva at hann veitir eigi tiþir at, sem mælt er.
oc varþar þeim manni skoggangr er við honom tekr. eþa tiþer
þiggr at honvm. eða samvistvm er við hann. Jafnt varþar samvista
við hann sem við skogarmann. lengr er lyriti er varit, at logbergi.
oc er þat fimtardoms sök. oc scal sok þa lysa at logbergi. oc heimta
hann sem aþra mans menn.[70]

(It is lawful for a man to have a priestling taught for his church.
He is to make an agreement with the boy himself if he is sixteen
winters old, but if he is younger, he is to make it with his legal
administrator. The whole agreement they make between them is
to be binding... If a priest absconds from the church for which he
was taught or absents himself so that he does not hold services as
prescribed, then the man who receives him into his home or hears
services from him or shares living quarters with him is liable to
full outlawry. The penalty for sharing living quarters with him is
the same as sharing with a full outlaw once it has been forbidden
by veto at Lögberg. It is a case for the Fifth Court and it is to be
published at Lögberg and the priest is to be claimed in the same
way as slaves.)

---

69 Einar Ól. Sveinsson in *ÍF* IV 1935, xiii. Björn Sigfússon in *KLNM* IV 1959, 104 and
references. Sigurður Líndal 1974, 249 ff.
70 *Grágás* Ia, 17-19.

The class of priests here mentioned had not achieved much standing. This text of *Grágás* cannot easily be dated, and there is thus no guarantee that its articles were all in force during the first years of Christianity. But all in all it is probable that the terms here meted out to priests had been settled before the Church was highly regarded and when the owners of churches were still all-powerful.[71] So we may suppose that the priests of Snorri Goði and his contemporaries did not enjoy much better conditions than the ones here stated – that they would be punished like runaway slaves if they abandoned their appointed task without leave. Such people were not likely to snatch away the power of the *goðar*, even though they took over from them the performance or certain religious ceremonies.

My chief conclusion from this study of sacrifices, assemblies and the office of the *goðar* in the tenth century is that the function of the *goðar* was many-sided, extending to matters later distinguished as religious or social. Both functions were a natural part of their duties, whether they were presiding over cases at assemblies or sacrifice in a cult-centre.

Translated by Joan Turville-Petre

---

71 Magnús Stefánsson 1975, 72 ff.

---

*This paper was read at a meeting of the Viking Society for Northern Research at University College London on February 3, 1984. It was originally published in *Temenos*, Vol. 21 1985, and in *Skírnir* 1985 and is published here with minor alterations.

Ágrip

Blót og þing. Hlutverk goðans á 10. öld

RITGERÐIN hefst á tilvísunum í *Hávamál* um eðli og inntak blótins, en síðan er birt og rædd hin fræga frásögn Snorra í *Hákonar sögu góða* af blóti Sigurðar Hlaðajarls og borin saman við frásögn *Eyrbyggju* af blótum Þórólfs Mostrarskeggja. Niðurstaða af nákvæmum samanburði er sú, að frásögn Snorra sé fyllri, ítarlegri og eldri en frásögn *Eyrbyggju*. Þá eru rædd rök með og móti gagnrýni sem fram hafði komið á trúverðugleik frásagnar Snorra af blótinu á Hlöðum og komist að þeirri niðurstöðu að Snorri byggi frásögn sína að öllum líkindum á norrænum arfsögnum.

Í öðrum kafla ritgerðarinnar er samhengi blóts og þings tekið til sérstakrar athugunar. Höfð er hliðsjón af fræðilegri niðurstöðu sem sett var fram fyrir nokkrum áratugum, að örnefni á Íslandi sem feli í sér nafnliðina hof og þing gefi til kynna að ekki hafi verið beint samband á milli blóts og þings á tíundu öld. Þessi niðurstaða var á sínum tíma talin veigamikil röksemd til stuðnings þeirri skoðun að stjórnskipun Íslands hafi ekki átt sér trúarlegar rætur.

Gegn ofangreindri niðurstöðu er teflt fram þeirri staðreynd að blót voru ekki framin á sama árstíma og þingin voru háð. Blótin voru framkvæmd að vetrarlagi en þingin háð um sumur og því var þess ekki að vænta að sérstakir samkomustaðir blóta, hofin, væru á sömu stöðum og þingin. Þá er einnig vakin athygli á því að örnefnarannsóknir hafi verið skammt á veg komnar þegar umræddar niðurstöður um takmarkað samband hofa og þinga voru settar fram. Þær niðustöður verði því ekki lengur teknar sem haldbær rök gegn því að stjórnskipun Íslands hafi í öndverðu verið af trúarlegum rótum.

Í þriðja kafla ritgerðarinnar eru teknir til nákvæms samanburðar tveir kaflar úr fornritum sem greina frá hlutverki goðans í helgihaldi fyrir kristnitöku. Annars vegar er um að ræða lýsingu *Eyrbyggju* á hofi Þórólfs Mostrarskeggja og því sem þar fór fram, en hins vegar er grein úr hinum fornu Úlfljótslögum úr *Hauksbók Landnámu*.

Að gerðum smásmugulegum samanburði á blótlýsingunum tveimur er niðurstaðan á þessa leið:

Frásögn *Eyrbyggju* einkennist af ónákvæmni höfundar sem gjörþekkir ekki það sem hann er að greina frá. Virðist augljóst að hún sé byggð á bliknuðum arfsögnum.

Kaflinn úr Úlfljótslögum er með gerólíkum svip, einkennist af skýrum og skilmerkilega orðuðum lagafyrirmælum þar sem hvergi fer milli mála hvað átt er við. Niðurstaðan er sú að þar sé um fornan lagatexta að ræða, væntanlega frá tíundu öld.

Í niðurlagi ritgerðarinnar er vikið sérstaklega að kristnitökunni á Íslandi og leitast við að svara því hvernig goðaveldi með rætur í trúarlegum jarðvegi gat lifað hana af. Dregið er fram hvernig goðarnir breyttu trúarafstöðu sinni sjálfviljugir á grundvelli vitneskju sem aflað var eftir gamalkunnum leiðum sem þeirra trú og heimsmynd tók gildar. Þá eru einnig rakin dæmi úr heimildum sem sýna að goðarnir hafa sjálfir fyrstir manna átt frumkvæði að kirkjubyggingum í hinum nýja sið sem er sterk vísbending um trúarlegt hlutverk þeirra fyrir kristnitöku.

Allsherjarniðurstaða ritgerðarinnar er í fáum orðum á þá lund, að öll rök bendi til þess að hlutverk goðans í samfélagi tíundu aldar á Íslandi hafi verið tvíþætt og tekið jafnt til blóta annars vegar, en hins vegar til löggjafar og veraldlegra stjórnarstarfa.

A Piece of Horse Liver
and the Ratification of Law

I

Hákon, the foster-son of Aðalsteinn, was brought up in England in the Christian faith. He probably came to power in Norway in the fifth decade of the tenth century, and reigned there for nearly twenty years. When he fell at Storð on the isle of Fitjar in about 960, Eyvindr the Plagiarist composed a memorial lay in his honour; here he showed the king on his way to Valhǫll and described his favourable reception there. Several historical works tell of what happened from the time when the Christian candidate for the throne reached Norway, until the fallen king was buried in accordance with ancient rites. I will now review what these sources have to say, and try to show the part played by King Hákon in religious affairs, as far as this is possible.

The fullest account of the religious conflicts between Hákon and his followers is given in *Hákonar saga góða* in *Heimskringla*. I will consider separately Snorri's methods and how he selected from the material he conceivably had to choose from, after I have discussed other works that deal with King Hákon.

Works dealing with Hákon's religious views and the government of his realm are (in chronological order, as far as this is ascertained):

1. *Hákonarmál*, the memorial lay that Eyvindr the Plagiarist composed about Hákon soon after his fall, by all accounts before 970. The whole poem is given in *Hákonar saga góða* in *Heimskringla,* some stanzas also in *Fagrskinna*.
2. *Historia Norwegiæ*, written 1152-1210.
3. *Ágrip af Nóregskonunga sǫgum*, composed c. 1190.
4. *Fagrskinna/Nóregs konunga tal*, probably written 1220-1230.
5. *Heimskringla* by Snorri Sturluson, composed c. 1230.

The value of these sources will be considered more fully when I come to specify what each source has to contribute of significance to the matter in hand.

II

In *Hákonarmál* Eyvindr the Plagiarist begins with Óðinn charging the valkyries with a mission: (st.1)

Gǫndul ok Skǫgul	Gǫndul and Skǫgul
sendi Gautatýr	did Gautatýr send
at kjósa of konunga,	to choose between kings,
hverr Yngva ættar	who of the race of Yngvi
skyldi með Óðni fara	was to join Óðinn
ok í Valhǫllu vesa.[1]	and enter Valhǫll.

Here at the outset the same note is struck as in *Eiríksmál*, the poem Queen Gunnhildr commissioned in memory of King Eiríkr, who fell in 954.[2] The pattern of both these memorial lays is the same; the king is invited to Valhǫll to augment the troop of champions with his own followers. But the difference between the poems is that Eiríkr sets out for Valhǫll as for an expected rendezvous, whereas Hákon hesitates and is not entirely sure of himself.

The general drift of *Hákonarmál* is briefly as follows. Sts 2-9 describe the valkyries setting out for the field of battle and observing the course of the fight. In st.10 it is said in so many words that Hákon had been invited to Valhǫll:

Gǫndul þat mælti	Gǫndul spoke thus
studdisk geirskapti:	leaning upon her spear-shaft:
"Vex nú gengi goða,	"The troop of the gods increases,
es Hákoni hafa	now that Hákon
með her mikinn	with his great army
heim bǫnd of boðit."	is made welcome to the gods."

Hákon heard this and was not entirely satisfied, but Skǫgul reminded him that the valkyries had often granted him victory (sts 11-12). The valkyries now rode to Valhǫll and told Óðinn that the

1 *ÍF* XXVI, 193.
2 *ÍF* XXVI, 154.

king was on his way; and Óðinn sent Hermóðr and Bragi to receive him (sts 13-14). St. 15 describes the feelings of Hákon on arriving at Valhǫll:

Ræsir þat mælti,	The prince spoke,
vas frá rómu kominn,	he had come from battle,
stóð allr í dreyra drifinn:	besmeared all in blood:
„Illúðigr mjǫk	"Most distrustful
þykkir oss Óðinn vesa.	does Óðinn seem.
Séumk vér hans of hugi."	I fear his intentions."

The fear felt by King Hákon is an indication that he had not been true to Óðinn all his life. But Bragi encourages the king, saying that the champions will grant him truce, and that his eight brothers are already present in Valhǫll (st.16). Hákon is still wary, and will not lay down his weapons and those of his men (st.17). But it is fair to say that by st. 18 the ancient gods are reconciled with Hákon, as follows:

Þá þat kynndisk,	Then was made known
hvé sá konungr hafði	how well the king
vel of þyrmt véum,	had respected holy shrines,
es Hákon báðu	when the gods and mighty powers
heilan koma	saluted Hákon
ráð ǫll ok regin.	with full welcome.

To "respect the shrines" means to spare sacred places, and the phrase presumably refers to the years when Hákon was a Christian. The poet appears to have evidence that he had destroyed neither temples nor shrines in those years, and when he comes to Valhǫll he is rewarded for his leniency.

The three last verses of *Hákonarmál* express the praise of Hákon, and the poem closes with the lines:

Síz Hákon fór	Since Hákon joined
með heiðin goð	the heathen gods
mǫrg es þjóð of þjáð (st.21).	many suffer oppression.

In these closing words there is again an allusion to the fact that after death Hákon went to join the ancient gods. In other words, he believed in these gods when he was killed, and they took him to themselves in full accord that he was a sincere believer. It is also implied that Hákon practised the ancient religion during his reign. Eyvindr the Plagiarist, author of the poem, was the great-grandson of Haraldr Finehair and therefore a kinsman of King Hákon. He took part in the king's last battle, fighting side by side with him. *Hákonarmál* can therefore be regarded as a very reliable authority on the king, his activities and his outlook in the last days of his life. Of course we must allow that the poet did not stint his praise of the king; but it seems highly improbable that he would attribute to him religious views which all contemporaries of King Hákon knew to be untrue.

Hákonarmál is believed to be preserved little altered or not at all from Eyvindr's original version.[3]

III

Now for what *Historia Norwegiæ* has to say about the reign of King Hákon and his religious belief:

> Hacon a maritimis Norwegiæ gentibus rex assumitur. Hic a chris- tianissimo rege in Anglia officiosissime educatus in tantum erro- rum incurrit, ut miserima communatione æterno transitorium præponeret regnum ac detinendæ dignitatis cura (proh dolor) apostata factus, idolorum servituti subactus, diis et non deo ser- viret. Qui quamvis labilis regni cæca ambitione a durabili digni- tate æternaliter labefactus, cunctis tamen in paganismo degentibus diligentius leges patrias et scita plebis observabat regibus. Ob hoc quidem principibus carus, vulgo devotus, XXVII annis suam hereditariam strenuissime defensabat patriam.[4]

> (Hákon was accepted as king by the coastal people of Norway. This man, dutifully reared in England by a most Christian king, fell into so great error that by wretched exchange he preferred the transitory to the eternal kingdom, and for the sake of maintaining his rank became alas! an apostate, and in thrall to idol-served gods instead of God. Who, although he was forever despoiled of lasting

---

3 Holm-Olsen in *KLNM* VI 1961, 50-51 and references.
4 Storm, *Monumenta*, 106.

honours through blind ambition of transient honours, yet nevertheless he maintained native laws and the customs of the people more assiduously than all the kings living in pagan times. For this reason he was a favourite with the chieftains and popular with the common people, and for 27 years he valiantly upheld his patrimony).

There follows an account of struggles against the sons of Gunnhildr, and finally the scene where Hákon had won victory, when a young man among the fugitives turned back, threw a spear that struck the king, and wounded him mortally. *Historia Norwegiæ* puts it like this:

> Quod factum divina ultione tali eventu accidisse lippis et tonsoribus liquido apparet, ubi puerum Christum denegare ausus hic divictis hostibus ab ignobili puero devinceretur.[5]

> (It plainly appeared to one and all that this event was a punishment from God, when a man who dared to deny the child Christ was himself overcome by a boy of low degree, just as he had defeated the enemy.)

There is much obscurity about the composition and sources of *HN*; the date of composition has been placed to 1152-1210. Scholars consider that the author's sources were both oral and written, and it is noteworthy that *HN* is not related to Icelandic historical works. Anne Holtsmark has pointed out that there is no reason to think that *HN* is always wrong when it diverges from other works of history. *HN* has had no perceptible influence on other works, although it has to some extent used the same sources as the Norwegian and Icelandic historians who were writing in the late twelfth and early thirteenth century.[6]

The author of *HN* was a learned man, well read by the standards of his time. He knew the Augustinian doctrine of the two kingdoms, the kingdom of God and the kingdom of this world; he accuses King Hákon of choosing the latter. He declares in so many

---

5   Storm, *Monumenta,* 107.
6   Holtsmark in *KLNM* VI 1961, 585-7; see further Ulset 1983, 16 ff.; 44 ff. and Ellehøj 1965, 142 ff.

words that Hákon had become an apostate, serving gods and not God. He gives us to understand that this occurred at the beginning of Hákon's reign, for he afterwards says that he held power for 27 years. Certain scholars have argued that Hákon did not reign for so long, suggesting that he came to power in the middle of the fifth decade and died c. 960-961. He would therefore have only reigned for approximately 15-18 years. A similar lack of certainty regarding the precise length of Hákon's reign is echoed in *Ágrip, Fagrskinna* and *Heimskringla*.[7]

HN gives Hákon full credit for respecting ancient laws and agreements, far better than other heathen kings had done. But as the author of HN saw it, the apostate must get his due requital, which awaited him when a low-born youth aimed his dart at the king who was pursuing fugitives after the battle at Fitjar. HN says nothing of the king's funeral rites.

IV

Ágrip af Nóregskonunga sǫgum has the following account of Hákon's reign in Norway:

> En Hákon sat þá einn konungr at Nóregi, ok var Nóregr svá góðr undir hans ríki, at hann var eigi munaðr betri fyr útan þat, at eigi var kristni á. En hann var kristinn ok átti konu heiðna ok veik mjǫk af kristninni fyr hennar sakir ok fyr vildar sakir við lýðinn, er á mót stóð kristninni, helt þó sunnudags helgi ok frjádaga fǫstu...
> Á hans dǫgum snǫrusk margir menn til kristni af vinsældum hans, en sumir hǫfnuðu blótum, þótt eigi kristnaðisk. Hann reisti nekkverar kirkjur í Nóregi ok setti lærða mann at. En þeir brenndu kirkjurnar ok vágu prestana fyrir hónum, svát hann mátti eigi því halda fyr illvirkjum þeira. Ok þar eptir gerðu Þrændir fǫr at hónum á Mærini ok báðu hann blóta sem aðra konunga í Nóregi, "ella rekum vér þik af ríki, nema þú gerir nekkvern hlut í samþykki eptir oss." En fyr því at hann sá ákafa þeira á hǫnd hónum at hǫfðingja ráði, þá snøri hann svá til at hann fyrkvað eigi í nekkverum hlut í yfirbragði til vingunar við þá. Svá er sagt, at hann biti á hrosslifr, ok svá, at hann brá dúki umb ok beit eigi bera, en blótaði eigi ǫðruvís. En svá er sagt, at síðan gekk hónum

---

7   Bjarni Aðalbjarnarson in *ÍF* XXVI 1941, xciif.; Bjarni Einarsson in *ÍF* XXIX 1984, viiff.; lxxff.

allt þyngra en áðr. Hann setti Golaþingslǫg eptir ráðagørð Þorleifs spaka, er verit hafði forðum.[8]

(Hákon then reigned as sole king of Norway; and Norway was so fruitful under his rule that the land was never more fortunate, but for the fact that it was not Christian. But he was Christian and had a heathen wife; he forsook Christianity chiefly for her sake and in favour of the people, who were opposed to Christianity, yet he observed Sundays and the Friday fast... In his time many people were converted through his popularity, and some gave up heathen worship although they did not take baptism. He built some churches in Norway and appointed men of learning to them. But the people burned the churches and killed the priests, so that he could not continue because of their depredations. Thereupon the people of Þrandheimr attacked him at Mærr and told him to sacrifice as other kings of Norway did - "or we will drive you from the throne, unless you go some way to meet our wishes." So because he realised their fury against him at the instigation of the chieftains, he gave way to the extent of not refusing an outward show here and there to gain their good graces. It is said that he took a bite of horse liver, wrapping it in a cloth without touching it directly; otherwise he did not take part in worship. But rumour goes that afterwards all went harder with him than before. He drew up the Law of the Gulaþing, which had been in force before, in consultation with Þorleifr the Wise.)

Next is the statement that Hákon reigned in peace for 15 years, after which he had to endure warfare with the sons of Gunnhildr. In the final battle he had put his enemies to flight when a cook's boy turned back to hurl a dart into his army which mortally wounded the king. *Ágrip* describes the last hours of King Hákon:

En er konungrinn sá, at at hónum leið, þá iðraðisk hann mjǫk mótgerða við guð. Vinir hans buðu hónum at færa lík hans til Englands vestr ok jarða at kirkjum. "Ek em eigi þess verðr, kvað hann, svá lifða ek sem heiðnir menn í mǫrgu, skal mik ok fyr því svá jarða sem heiðna menn. Vætti ek mér þaðan af meiri miskunnar af guði sjálfum en ek sjá verðr," ok andaðisk á Hákonarhellu, en hann var heygðr á Sæheimi á Norðhǫrðalandi.[9]

8 *ÍF* XXIX, 8-9.
9 *ÍF* XXIX, 11.

(And when the king saw that he was near death, he deeply repented of his offences against God. His friends offered to carry his body west to England and give it church burial. "I am not worthy of that," said he. "In many ways I have lived like the heathens, therefore I should be buried like the heathens. In this way I could hope for greater mercy than I deserve at God's hands." He died at Hákonarhella, and was buried at Sæheimr in North Hǫrðaland.)

Ágrip is dated c. 1190, or shortly after.[10] Bjarni Aðalbjarnarson in his time reckoned that the author of *Ágrip* relied principally on the following sources: the work of the monk Thedoric (written 1177-1188); a Norwegian work in Latin which also would have been the source of *HN*; a lost saga of Hákon the Good; and Norwegian oral tradition, especially from Þrandheimr.[11]

Ágrip shows an attitude to King Hákon which differs completely from that of *HN* and *Hákonarmál*. There is strong emphasis on the Christianity of Hákon, and others are blamed for his backsliding. To begin with, it is stated that he had a heathen wife and for her sake turned away from Christianity, while observing Christian holidays. Later we hear that he converted people, stopped others from heathen worship, built churches and appointed priests. Because of the evil deeds of the heathens, he could not continue this work. The Þrandheimers are said to have attacked the king and threatened to drive him from the throne unless he made sacrifice; but Hákon wrapped horse liver in a cloth and bit upon it, without otherwise taking part in the ceremony. After that, everything went against him. The author of *Ágrip* encourages the view that King Hákon had been a tolerably good Christian in the last days of his life, humble and penitent and hoping for the mercy of Almighty God. Contradictory as it may seem, the author of *Ágrip* gives us to understand that it was this Christian humility that made King Hákon decide to be buried in accordance with the ancient rites.

---

10 Bjarni Einarsson in *ÍF* XXIX 1984, xi.
11 Bjarni Aðalbjarnarson 1936, 54; see further Ellehøj 1965, 197 ff. and Ulset 1983, 111 ff. where closer examination of the connection between *HN's* and *Ágrip's* texts is made.

V

Fagrskinna/Nóregs konunga tal gives this account of the reign of Há-kon the Good:

Hann var bæði vinsæll ok ársæll. Hann setti lǫg um allan Nóreg með ráði Þorleifs ens spaka ok annarra viturra manna, ok af þeim lǫgum nýtti enn helgi Ólafr konungr mestan hlut. Á enu sextánda ári ríkis átti hann fjǫlmennt þing inn í Þrándheimi á Mærini, ok á því þingi gǫrðu Þrændir konunginum tvá kosti, at hann skyldi blóta eptir vanða enna fyrri konunga ok fylla svá en fornu lǫg til árs ok friðar, ellegar mundu þeir reka hann af ríkinu, ef hann vildi [eigi] í þessu vera svá fyrir þeim sem um ríki ok skatttǫku. Konungr vildi þetta víst eigi gøra. Ástvinir konungs ok mikit fólk gengu í millum ok biðja bændr þyrmask við konung, ok tala þeir, hversu nytsamligr þeira hǫfðingi var sínum þegnum ok mikill ráðsmaður til laga ok siða. Í annan stað biðja þeir konung minnka þenna kurr ok taka einn lítinn hlut í samþykkt, svá at blótmenn kalli eigi at af hónum verði niðrfall laganna. Fyrir huggæðis sakir ok ástar við vini sína, þá gørði hann eptir bæn þeira ok blótaði.[12]

(He was both popular and lucky for the crops. He established laws throughout Norway on the advice of Þorleifr the Wise and other skilled men, and King Ólafr the Saint incorporated the greater part of these laws. In the sixteenth year of his reign he held a great assembly inland at Mærr; at this assembly the people of Þrand-heimr faced the king with alternatives: that he should worship according to the custom of past kings, thus ratifying the ancient laws governing fruitfulness and peace, or else they would drive him from the kingdom if he refused to be their leader in this respect as well as in government and the taking of tribute. The king decidedly would not comply. The king's close friends and many others intervened, asking the farmers to show forbearance and pointing out how beneficent their lord was to his thanes, how good a steward of laws and customs. On the other hand, they asked the king to quell this protest and take one little part in com-pliance, so that the heathens could not allege that he had caused abrogation of the law. In goodness of heart and love of his friends, he heard their plea and made sacrifice.)

---

12 *ÍF* XXIX, 80.

Fagrskinna goes on to deal with the later years of Hákon's reign and his struggles against the sons of Gunnhildur. There is a very full description of his last battle, quoting many verses from *Hákonarmál,* but no verse that attributes religious practices to Hákon. The conclusion of the story is very like that of *Ágrip;* the king is said to have repented in the hour of death of all he had done against God and the laws of Christendom. He declared that he was not worthy of church burial, and was greatly mourned by friends and foe alike.[13]

Fagrskinna is thought to be not earlier than 1220, not later than 1240. The most probable time of writing is 1220-1230. It is based to a great extent on earlier works, *Ágrip, Morkinskinna* and so on; but the author does not seem to have known *Heimskringla.*[14]

Fagrskinna has no word on any missionary activity of Hákon's, but is the first to mention that Hákon had been popular and lucky for the crops, and that he established laws over all Norway which were so well formulated that St. Ólafr was able to use the greater part of them. The author of *Fagrskinna* frames his narrative in such a way as to imply that King Hákon had been popular and lucky and established these good laws while he was still Christian. After this account, he states that in the sixteenth year of his reign the Þrandheimers confronted him with two choices at the assembly at Mærr: to worship after the custom of earlier kings "and so ratify the ancient laws for fruitfulness and peace", or they would drive him from the throne. The king refused to do this. Friends on both sides then stepped in, according to *Fagrskinna,* asking the farmers to bear with the king, and the king "to take one little part in compliance, so that the heathens could not allege that he had caused an abrogation of the law. Through the goodness of his heart and love of his friends, he heard their plea and made sacrifice."

The author of *Fagrskinna* is of the same mind as the author of *Ágrip* about the results of King Hákon taking part in worship, saying that God laid it on Hákon as a punishment for sacrificing that ever after his kingdom suffered attacks from the sons of Gunnhildr and other marauders.

---

13 *ÍF* XXIX, 86-94.

14 Halvorsen in *KLNM* IV 1959, 139 f.; Bjarni Einarsson in *ÍF* XXIX 1984, lxi ff. and references.

The author of *Fagrskinna* evidently had some difficulty in reconciling *Hákonarmál* with the image of Hákon he is creating. He certainly knew the poem, but quoted only those strophes dealing with the battles of Hákon's last campaign, as also the eulogy at the close of the poem. He omits all strophes alluding to Hákon's association with the Old Norse gods. Introducing the first strophes he quotes, he states that in the poem composed by Eyvindr after Hákon's fall, the scene where Óðinn invites him to Valhǫll is modelled on a similar passage in the lay commissioned by Gunnhildr for Eiríkr; thus he suggests that the relevant strophes in *Hákonarmál* tell us nothing much, since they are lifted from *Eiríksmál*.

The concluding words on Hákon in *Fagrskinna* are very similar to those of *Ágrip*. In the hour of death the king repents of all his offences against God and the laws of Christendom, thinks himself unworthy of burial in church and sends a "document" making over his retinue and all his realm to his kinsman Haraldr.

VI

Before we go further, I think it will be as well to sum up the main points in these sources, *Historia Norwegiæ*, *Ágrip* and *Fagrskinna*, and try to establish to what extent the material could derive from oral traditions of the tenth century rooted in Old Norse religion; and to what extent we can identify later oral traditions with a post-Conversion stamp and adjusted to the taste of Christian historians. It has already been indicated that strong Christian tendencies are apparent in all three works.

The argument of *Historia Norwegiæ* is simple: Hákon gave up everlasting bliss in the kingdom of God for transitory power in the kingdom of this world. The defection would seem to have occurred soon after Hákon reached Norway, or at the time when he was striving for power. Yet the king respected the laws of his forefathers and their agreements, and so gained the love of both chieftains and common people. But God's punishment was hanging over him, and it took the form of a young man who hurled a dart as the king was pursuing his defeated enemies. In this simple text the Church's sphere of thought emerges plainly; Augustine's doctrine of the Two Kingdoms comes to the fore, and the apostate receives his due recompense. On the other hand, the author of *Historia Norwegiæ* seems to have taken the fortunate rule of the apostate and his regard for the law from tenth-century traditions. Likewise, the young man who threw the fatal dart at the king will have come from this kind of source.

I conclude that the account of Hákon the Good in *Historia Norwegiæ* contains historical facts and tenth-century traditions, rendered in literary form by a man of learning.

Ágrip presents traditions that stress the Christianity of King Hákon, traditions that show signs of being formed and circulated after the Conversion. This material shows the worthy Christian king struggling against all odds in the face of evil heathens. In the end, they forced him to make sacrifice, but Hákon went no further than to chew a piece of horse liver that he first wrapped in a cloth. The author of *Ágrip* does not tell us when in Hákon's reign this incident occurred; but when the author of *Fagrskinna* comes to date the incident he names to the sixteenth year of Hákon's reign. This could be an effort to square two different sources: the account of Hákon's sacrifice on one hand, and on the other the statement that everything went harder with him than before.

Fagrskinna preserves a very significant factor in its account of Hákon's sacrifice. Here for the first time is the statement that the people of Þrándheimr confronted Hákon with two choices: "to worship according to the custom of former kings and thus ratify ancient laws for fruitfulness and peace, or else they would drive him from the throne." In this statement there seems to lurk an ancient formula expressing a close tie between sacrifice and lawgiving in northern lands. Not surprisingly, evidence of this linkage is hard to come by; but we may recall what Úlfljótr's Laws say about worship conducted by the Icelandic *goðar* at assemblies. Here the ring on which the holy oath was sworn is described:

> ... þann baug skyldi hverr goði hafa á hendi sér til lǫgþinga allra, þeira er hann skyldi sjálfr heyja, ok rjóða hann þar áðr í roðru nautsblóðs þess, er hann blótaði þar sjálfr. Hverr sá maðr, er þar þurfti lǫgskil af hendi at leysa at dómi, skyldi áðr eið vinna at þeim baugi...[15]

---

15 *ÍF* I, 313-315.

(... each *goði* should wear this ring on his arm at all established assemblies in which he himself should participate, and redden it beforehand in gore from the blood of the beast he personally sacrificed there. Everyone who needed to perform legal duties there at court should previously swear an oth on that ring.)

On the constitution of the tenth-century Icelandic Commonwealth, constitutional enactment and sacrifice were all of a piece, inseparably combined.[16] Once these ties had been snapped, breakdown, disorder, anarchy and lawlessness followed. This is what Þorgeir the Lawspeaker saw in his day, and this is why he acted quickly at the fatal moment, as the event showed.[17] There are other witnesses to this close link between law and religion in Iceland in the tenth century; here may be mentioned the account in *Víga-Glúms saga* of the sanction on Þverá, forbidding condemned men to stay there because the place was sacred to Freyr.[18] People who had broken the law were likewise excluded from the area enclosed by the sacred ropes of holy places.

In *Fagrskinna* this same close and unbreakable association between worship and law shows itself, and is emphasised again later in the same passage on the reason why Hákon let himself be persuaded to sacrifice: "so that the heathens could not allege that he had caused an abrogation of the law." Here it is plainly implied that two things were in balance: either the law of the land was ratified, or the country would be without law, with all the disasters that would follow. *Fagrskinna* is all the more reliable as a source because the author is not describing the manners and customs of tenth-century Norway; he seeks only to justify King Hákon for adopting the impious expedient of making sacrifice. He did it to ratify the law and to guarantee that the country had laws. In other words, he sacrificed his eternal welfare - as the author of *Fagrskinna* apparently saw it - in favour of transitory welfare for his followers.

This work therefore seems to me to bring home to us the fact that in the tenth century there survived a sacral kingship in which

---

16 Strömbäck 1975, 41; Jón Hnefill Aðalsteinsson 1985a, 33, and 1997a, 163-187.
17 Jón Hnefill Aðalsteinsson 1978, 97 ff.
18 *ÍF* IX, 66.

sacrifice and law formed a living whole, neither able to exist without the other. In the light of this, it is also understandable that the Norsemen of the time would not venture to take a king who practised a religion differing from that of his followers. The law was simply not ratified unless the highest authority in the kingdom sacrificed in association with acceptance of the laws. He sealed or confirmed it by sacrifice. Hákon understood this, and so he had but one way to power, to put up with the horse liver so that the law would be ratified and the kingdom remain intact. This interpretation of *Fagrskinna's* text accords very well with both *Hákonarmál* and *Historia Norwegiæ*, both of which imply that Hákon turned from Christianity to Old Norse religion once he came to power in Norway, and kept to that faith ever after until the end of his life. Under the influence of Christian hagiography, *Ágrip* and *Fagrskinna* attempt to defend the king, excuse his apostasy and blame it on others; but try as they may, the older attitude to the apostasy of the king and his function in worship still shows through.

A great deal has been written about sacral kingship.[19] There is little dispute among scholars that Norse kings were divine to some extent, but this feature could take various forms.[20] The king as such could be considered of divine descent; this applied to all kings who traced their ancestry to the Ynglings of Sweden and thence to Freyr and Njǫrðr. Hákon the Good also belonged to this line. Secondly, the king took a direct part in worship and himself offered sacrifice. This is recorded of many kings. Thirdly, it was possible to sacrifice the king himself; the best-known examples are Dómaldi and apparently Ólafr the Wood-carver in Sweden. The reason for resorting to this expedient was that the king had disappointed his followers. He had not been attended by the luck or fruitfulness which a king was in duty bound to supply to his followers, by virtue of his office as a leader of the people bearing fertility and good fortune.[21]

---

19 See Turville-Petre 1964, 190-5; de Vries 1956, 393-6 and the works there cited.
20 McTurk 1976, 139 ff.
21 Ström 1959, 702 ff.; Höfler 1959, 664 ff.

VII

Continuing this subject, it is interesting to see what Snorri Sturluson has made of the material here considered. Clearly *Hákonarmál* and *Ágrip* were among the sources available to Snorri, and perhaps also *Fagrskinna*. It is more doubtful that he had access to *Historia Norwegiæ*.

In *Hákonar saga góða*, Snorri gives a full account of the reign of Hákon the Good in Norway and his quarrels with the Norwegians on differences of religion. The account begins:

> Hákon konungr var vel kristinn, er hann kom í Nóreg. En fyrir því at þar var land allt heiðit ok blótskapr mikill ok stórmenni mart, en hann þóttisk liðs þurfa mjǫk ok alþýðuvinsæld, þá tók hann þat ráð at fara leynilega með kristninni... Hann ætlaði svá, er hann festisk í landinu...at hafa þá fram kristniboð... Kom svá með vinsæld hans, at margir létu skírask, en sumir létu af blótum... En er Hákon konungr þóttisk fengit hafa styrk af nǫkkurum ríkismǫnnum at halda upp kristninni, þá sendi hann til Englands eptir byskupi ok ǫðrum kennimǫnnum. Ok er þeir kómu í Nóreg, þá gerði Hákon konungr þat bert, at hann vildi bjóða kristni um allt land. En Mærir ok Raumdælir skutu þannug máli sínu sem Þrændir váru ... Þeir svara svá, at þeir vilja þessu máli skjóta til Frostaþings...[22]

(King Hákon was a good Christian when he came to Norway. But the whole country was heathen, idolatry was rife and the aristocracy were numerous, while he felt in need of support and popular approval; therefore he decided to keep quiet about his Christianity ... He intended, when he had a foothold in the country... to start upon a mission ... His popularity was such that many were baptized, and some gave up heathen worship... So when King Hákon judged that he had the support of some counsellors to maintain Christianity, he sent to England for a bishop and other teachers. When these arrived in Norway, King Hákon made it public that he meant to preach Christianity throughout the land. But the people of Mærr and Raumdalr passed their dilemma on to the people of Þrandheimr... They replied that they wished to refer the matter to the assembly of Frosta...)

---

22 *ÍF* XXVI, 169-170.

In the next chapter Snorri produces his famous description of the heathen ceremony held by Sigurðr Earl of Hlaðir; later he turns to the occasion when King Hákon arrived at the assembly of Frosta and announced that he required all men to be baptized and relinquish heathen rites and the ancient faith. The spokesman of the farmers rejected the king's proposal, saying that if he meant...

> "...at deila afli ok ofríki við oss, þá hǫfum vér bændr gǫrt ráð várt, at skiljask allir við þik ok taka oss annan hǫfðingja, þann er oss haldi til þess at vér megim í frelsi hafa þann átrúnað, sem vér viljum. Nú skaltu, konungr, kjósa um kosti þessa, áðr þing sé slitit."

> ("...to use force and oppression against us, then we farmers have determined all to break away from you and choose another prince who will rule us in such a way that we can hold in freedom the belief we desire. Sire, you must make your choice before the assembly is dissolved.")

Earl Sigurðr answered for the king, saying that he wished to keep on friendly terms with the farmers. They then said that they wanted him to sacrifice for fruitfulness and peace for them all; and Earl Sigurðr advised the king to do what the farmers wished. What happened at the Hlaðir sacrificial feast is then related. The king made the sign of the cross over the toast, and went as far as to inhale the steam of the horsemeat-stew once he had draped a linen cloth over the handle of the cauldron. The same winter the farmers rose in full rebellion against Hákon's Christianity, killing priests and burning churches he had built. But now the time had come for the Yule feast in Mærr, and the king and Earl Sigurðr arrived there:

> Inn fyrsta dag at veizlunni veittu bændr honum atgǫngu ok báðu hann blóta, en hétu honum afarkostum ella. Sigurðr jarl bar þá mál í millum þeira. Kømr þá svá, at Hákon konungr át nǫkkura bita af hrosslifr. Drakk hann þá ǫll minni krossalaust, þau er bændr skenktu honum.[23]

> (On the first day of the festival the farmers gathered against him and commanded him to make sacrifice, threatening rough treatment otherwise. Earl Sigurðr arbitrated between them. It came to

---

23 *ÍF* XXVI, 172.

the point that King Hákon ate some bites of horse liver. Then he drank all the toasts given him by the farmers without signing them with the cross.)

The king uttered threats against the Þrandheimers when he left the festival and...

... var svá reiðr, at ekki mátti orðum við hann koma.[24]

(...was so angry that no one could say a word to him.)

Earl Sigurðr warned the King not to make war against the people of his country. When hostilities broke out soon after, Earl Sigurðr came to meet King Hákon with a large army:

Váru þar þá allir Þrændir, þeir er um vetrinn hǫfðu mest gengit at konunginum at pynda hann til blóta. Váru þeir þá allir í sætt teknir af fortǫlum Sigurðar jarls.[25]

(There were present all the men of Þrandheimr, those who over the winter had pressed hardest to make the king sacrifice under duress. All of them were now brought into agreement by the persuasions of Earl Sigurðr.)

Here I have touched on the main points only of the religious dispute between Hákon the Good and the Þrandheimers, as Snorri depicts it in *Heimskringla*. According to him, the origin of the matter was that Hákon was a Christian when he came to the throne in Norway, and had set his heart on converting the country. He thought of moving cautiously to start with, and of going full out when he had gathered round himself a strong following of Christians. Yet he seems to have been too hasty or to have misjudged the opposition to Christianity in the country, for by gradual degrees he had to give way to the people of Þrandheimr. According to Snorri's account, the one thing the Þrandheimers insisted on was freedom to manage their religious affairs. Thus a conflict arose, in which the will of Hákon to establish Christianity in Norway had to yield to

---

24 *ÍF* XXVI, 173.
25 *ÍF* XXVI, 173.

the will of the Norwegian chieftains to carry on with their ancient religion in peace. Snorri presents this dispute with brilliance. Hákon gives way bit by bit, from the moment when he inhales the steam of the horse-stew until at last he is forced to take some bites of horse liver. It is scarcely possible to imagine how the process could be better expressed than it is here. Snorri has raised the account of these wrangles into classic literature.

After telling of the reconciliation with the Þrandheimers, Snorri alludes no more to the Christianity of King Hákon. Once he had come off victorious in the struggle already mentioned, he passed detailed laws on the defence of the land and reigned well-loved a bare twenty years: "Var þá ok árferð góð í landi ok góðr friðr."[26] (Then there were good harvests in the land and good peace.) After this there followed some years of turmoil, ending with the fall of Hákon in battle. His friends laid him in a howe, and then:

> Mæltu þeir svá fyrir grepti hans sem heiðinna manna siðr var til, vísuðu honum til Valhallar. Eyvindr skáldaspillir orti kvæði eitt um fall Hákonar konungs ok svá þat, hversu honum var fagnat.[27]

> (They made speeches before his grave in the heathen fashion, speeding him on his way to Valhǫll. Eyvindr the Plagiarist composed a poem on the fall of King Hákon and the welcome given him.)

Snorri Sturluson's account of Hákon the Good and his struggles with the Þrandheimers, judging by such sources he had available, gives a fair idea of Snorri himself and his methods of work. His estimate of his sources is plain. *Hákonarmál* stands foremost; he never flatly contradicts the poem in his description of events. This observation accords very well with what Snorri himself says in the prologue to *Heimskringla*: that poems were the most reliable sources to be had, and that a poet had to guard against an idle word in an elegy just as much as in the poem recited before the prince in person.[28] Snorri steers clear of hagiographic material in *Ágrip* and

---

26 *ÍF* XXVI, 176.
27 *ÍF* XXVI, 193.
28 *ÍF* XXVI, 6. On Snorri's use of poems in historical works, see Sigurður Nordal 1973, 137ff.

Fagrskinna; he proceeds as if it did not exist. On the other hand, he enlarges somewhat on Hákon's mission; it has been observed that this account greatly resembles that of the mission of Ólafr Tryggva-son.[29] But in this rendering Hákon's mission acquires a marked enhancement and suspense. Hákon moves step by step until he makes a decisive push. Snorri skilfully describes the head-on clash when Hákon comes up against opposition from the farmers' leaders. This description is literature of timeless value; here Snorri is presenting struggles that might as well have taken place in his own day. One incident that springs to mind is the time when St. Þorlákr brought the archbishop's decree to Iceland, and came into collison with Jón Loftsson, Snorri's foster-father on the occasion of the dedication of Höfðabrekka church.[30] More such stories could be quoted, but this was a quarrel fully understood by Snorri's contemporaries and one after their own hearts.

As I mentioned earlier, it is not clear whether Snorri knew *Fagrskinna*. But if he did know that work, the question arises why he said nothing of the abrogation of law which would follow if King Hákon had refused outright to make sacrifice. Did Snorri really not know of the value of the sacrificial ceremony in connection with the law; or did he think it a less interesting narrative topic than the skilful setting that he created for the quarrels between Hákon the Good and the Þrandheimers: It is hard to find any satisfactory answer; but it is appropriate to recall what has been written on Snorri's handling of the historical material available to him. Sigurð-ur Nordal in his day did justice to Snorri's working method in this field, and here is his judgment:

> Snorri ber nú í þessu efni mjög af öllum þeim sagnariturum, sem færðust í fang að steypa saman skrifuðum heimildum. Yfirsýn hans er svo skýr, hann er svo viss í því að setja efni fram í réttri tímaröð og gæta fulls samræmis, að hann strandar aldrei á þeim skerjum, sem liggja í augum uppi.[31]

> (In this matter Snorri towers far above all those historians who undertook the task of combining written sources. His survey is so

---

29 Bjarni Aðalbjarnarson in *ÍF* XXVI, lxxxix.
30 *Oddaverja þáttr* 1953, 136-7.
31 Sigurður Nordal 1973, 151.

penetrating, he presents the material in chronological order and due proportion with so sure a touch that he never runs aground on those reefs which are plain to see.)

In *Hákonar saga góða* this skill is seen to good effect, and Snorri faultlessly disposes the material in a classical literary form. But it seems as if, precisely because of this artistic emphasis, an important religious motif has got lost. We should keep this point in mind when we evaluate other works of Snorri's touching on Old Norse religion and Old Norse mythology. The upshot might well be that Snorri, when all is said and done, was greater as a literary artist than as a mythologist.

On the other hand, Snorri makes a good case for the divine origin of the Norse kings. In *Ynglinga saga* he traces royal houses right back to the mythological Njǫrðr and Freyr and straight through to the historic kings of Sweden, Denmark and Norway who all had roots in mythological prehistory. He states that Njǫrðr and Freyr had been popular and good for the crops, and that Freyr retained these attributes after death. The Swedes:

> ... kǫlluðu hann veraldargoð [ok] blótuðu hann mest til árs ok friðar alla ævi síðan.[32]

> (...called him god of the world and worshipped him especially for good crops and peace ever thereafter.)

The descendants of the divine kings kept these attributes as time went on, according to Snorri, and many got the reputation of being good for the crops. But if, like Dómaldi, they lost this faculty, they themselves were sacrificed for fertility.[33] The concept of the king's popularity and his fertility-value passed on into Christian historiography without comment and apparently without the authors always realising that they were using an idea taken from Old Norse religion. *Ágrip* says that Norway was so fortunate under the rule of Hákon that prosperity had never been greater, except for the fact that there was no Christian religion. There is no mention here of popularity or fertility, but the idea is the same. On the other hand,

---

32 *ÍF* XXVI, 25.
33 *ÍF* XXVI, 32.

Fagrskinna applies the ancient formula to Hákon: "Hann var bæði vinsæll ok ársæll."[34] (He was both popular and good for the crops.) It is interesting that the author of *Fagrskinna* here uses the age-old formula of Old Norse religion without any comment, probably not realising what was implied in its old religious sense. The expression used in Snorri's *Hákonar saga góða* is not unlike this, for he says of Hákon's reign after he had taken part in the worship at Mærr: "En Hákon konungr réð Nóregi ok var inn vinsælasti. Var þá ok góð árferð í landi ok góðr friðr."[35] (And King Hákon ruled over Norway and was very popular. There were good harvests in the country and good peace.)

Here are the same attributes as those of Freyr in ancient Sweden. Hákon the Good seems to have acted as an intermediary between the world of men and the world of gods no less than Freyr did. Traditions about this part of his royal function had most probably already taken shape in the tenth century, at a time when nobody had any doubt that the king's capacity to bring good crops and his popularity were a direct result of his fidelity to the ancient gods and his worship of them. And this element of heathen piety in the kingship of the apostate Hákon (originally closely associated with the ancient gods) survived the change of religion and emerges to some extent in three historical works, *Ágrip, Fagrskinna* and *Hákonar saga góða*.

VIII

Finally, it is as well to summarise the main points which have been discussed above.

1. The documents on Hákon the Good, King of Norway, differ in age and reliability. The poem *Hákonarmál* is the oldest and most trustworthy. *Historia Norwegiæ* seems to use historical facts which the learned author interprets. *Ágrip* and *Fagrskinna* emphasise Hákon's Christianity, and include hagiographic material which must have been formulated after the Conversion. But both of these works also contain ancient motifs originating in the tenth century.

---

34 *ÍF* XXIX, 80.
35 *ÍF* XXVI, 176.

2. In *Hákonar saga góða,* Snorri on the one hand values *Hákonarmál* above all, discarding late hagiographic matter about the Christian inclinations of the king. On the other hand, Snorri is chiefly concerned to give artistic form to his historical material, and in this process an important mythological motif is lost; it survives in *Fagrskinna* alone. This motif bears every sign of representing what actually happened in the tenth century, when the Old Norse religion was in full vigour.

3. When the sources have been compared and evaluated, it seems most probable that King Hákon arrived in Norway a Christian and met strong opposition from Norwegian chieftains because of his religion. Therefore he turned to the Old Norse religion when he came to the throne, and upheld that faith from that time on.

4. The basic disagreement in religious matters between Hákon the Good and the Þrandheimers apparently arose because the laws of the land could not be ratified unless the king gave them the seal of sacrifice.

Translated by Joan Turville-Petre

---

*This paper was read at the Snorrastefna conference in Reykjavík, on July 25-27 1990. It was originally published in "Snorrastefna", *Rit Stofnunar Sigurðar Nordals* 1, 1992, Reykjavík.

Ágrip

Biti af hrosslifur og landslög staðfest

HÁKON Aðalsteinsfóstri var kristinn er hann braust til valda í Noregi á fyrri hluta 10. aldar, en er hann féll um 960 var hann heygður að fornum sið. Í erfikvæði um Hákon og nokkrum sagnaritum er skýrt frá sinnaskiptum konungsins á mismunandi hátt. Heimildirnar eru: *Hákonarmál* eftir Eyvind skáldaspilli, ort fyrir 970, *Historia Norwegiæ*, rituð 1152-1210, *Ágrip af Nóregskonunga sǫgum*, samin nálægt 1190, *Fagrskinna - Nóregs konunga tal*, líklega samin 1220-1230 og loks *Hákonar saga góða* í *Heimskringlu*, sem Snorri Sturluson ritaði um 1230.

Heimildirnar um Hákon konung góða eru mismunandi bæði að aldri og áreiðanleik. *Hákonarmál* eru að sjálfsögðu traustasta heimildin, enda samtímamaður konungs sem þar segir frá atvikum í bundnu máli sem talið er að lítt eða ekki hafi raskast í geymd. Meginniðurstaða *Hákonarmála* er sú að Hákon góði hafi virt helgidóma norrænnar trúar og honum hafi verið fagnað í Valhöll eftir andlátið. Frá kristni konungs segir ekkert sérstaklega í kvæðinu.

Historia Norwegiæ leggur megináherslu á fráhvarf Hákonar frá kristinni trú, sem samkvæmt þessari heimild virðist hafa gerst við valdatöku hans. Höfundur *HN* segir síðan að konungur hafi ríkt farsællega í áratugi og haldið vel lög landsins, en að lokum hafi honum hefnst fyrir fráhvarfið og það valdið falli hans. *HN* virðist að miklu leyti fara með sögulegar staðreyndir um Hákon góða, en þær eru túlkaðar í anda kristinnar kenningar af lærðum höfundi.

Ágrip og *Fagrskinna* leggja áherslu á kristni Hákonar og birta helgisagnaefni sem hlýtur að hafa mótast eftir kristnitöku. Í báðum þessum ritum eru þó einnig forn minni sem að líkindum má rekja til tíundu aldar. Er þar merkast það sem *Fagrskinna* segir um að Hákon hafi blótað til þess að ekki yrði sagt að hann hindraði að landslög tækju gildi. Þessi frásögn er heimild um náin tengsl laga og blóta á tíundu öld í helgu konungdæmi á Norðurlöndum.

Í *Hákonar sögu góða* sækir Snorri mest til *Hákonarmála* en hafnar helgisagnaefni um kristilegt hugarfar Hákonar konungs. Snorra virðist þó mest í mun að setja efni sitt fram í listrænum búningi og við það glatast mikilvægt trúarsögulegt minni um náin tengsl blóts og laga, minni sem *Fagrskinna* ein hefur varðveitt.

Þegar heimildir hafa verið metnar og bornar saman virðist líklegast að Hákon góði hafi komið til Noregs kristinn, en mætt sterkri andstöðu hjá norskum höfðingjum vegna trúar sinnar. Því hafi hann snúist til norrænnar trúar við valdatöku sína og haldið þá trú æ síðan.

Meginágreiningur Hákonar góða og Þrænda vegna trúmála virðist hafa átt rætur að rekja til þess, að landslög tóku ekki gildi nema konungur innsiglaði þau með blóti.

POSTSCRIPT

A PIECE OF HORSE LIVER AND THE RATIFICATION OF LAW was first presented at the "Snorrastefna" Conference on Snorri Sturluson held in Reykjavík on 25th-27th July 1990, and was published in *Rit Stofnunar Sigurðar Nordals* I, 1992.[36] Several of the critics who have discussed this book have made special mention of this article. Gerd Wolfgang Weber, for example, takes up my suggestion that Snorri's emphasis on artistic form resulted in the loss of certain important religious details. He believes Snorri *did* retain the religious element concerning the connection between the law and religious belief in *Hákonar saga góða*, even though it is not directly stated in Snorri's description of the sacrificial ceremony in chs 17-18. Weber argues that in his description of the political situation in Norway given in chs 15-20 of *Hákonar saga góða*, Snorri gives a clear explanation of the changes that will take place if the farmers are forced to replace the old pagan law with the new Christian one. This detailed report shows that Snorri was well aware of what was at stake.[37] In support of this argument, Weber refers to his detailed typological study of the conversion of Northern Europe and Scandinavia which was published in 1987.[38]

Bearing in mind Weber's reasoning, I am quite ready to accept that Snorri knew about the inseparable connection between the law and religious ritual, and the legal necessity that the king should ratify the law by taking part in the sacrifice. Nonetheless, the fact that Snorri makes an obvious decision not to outline this relationship in any clear sense seems to me to be a strong indication that he did not regard it as being his role to explain ancient pagan rituals.

---

36 Úlfar Bragason, ed. 1992. *Snorrastefna. Rit Stofnunar Sigurðar Nordals* I. Rvík, 81-98.
37 Weber 1994, 124-125.
38 Weber 1987, 111-125.

Sacrilege in a Marital Bed

THE SAGAS of Icelanders as sources of Old Norse religious belief are obscure and difficult to handle. So to begin with I shall run through some main themes of the research carried out during the last decades, and refer to leading experts on the origin and nature of Icelandic saga-writing.

It is some fifty years since Sigurður Nordal wrote the introduction to his edition of *Egils saga* in the series *Íslenzk fornrit*. This introduction set the standard for this admirable series of texts, and many of the chief ideas characteristic of the so-called "Icelandic School"[1] have been published there. In his introduction, Nordal reviewed (among other things) the differing opinions held by older scholars on the part authors took in the composition of sagas, and he added:

> Þó er það almennt viðurkennt, að í öllum hinum eldri sögum sé meginefnið sótt í munnlegar frásögur, en margar sögur beri það hins vegar með sér, að vera fyrst færðar saman í heild af riturunum, svo að ekki sé talað um þær sögur, sem eru að mestu eða öllu leyti skáldskapur.[2]

> (It is generally recognised that most of the material in all the older sagas comes from oral accounts, yet many sagas clearly show that they were first formed as a whole by their authors, not to mention those sagas that are entirely or mostly fictitious.)

Nordal next attacked the doctrine that the Sagas of Icelanders for the most part reflect a fully-formed oral tradition, saying:

> ... mín eigin niðurstaða, af athugun einstakra sagna og þróun íslenzkrar sagnaritunar yfirleitt, er í stuttu máli sú, að engin saga, sem vér þekkjum nú, sé í letur færð í sömu mynd og hún hefur

---

1 Jón Hnefill Aðalsteinsson 1991: "Íslenski skólinn", *Skírnir*, 103-129 and works cited there.
2 Sigurður Nordal in *ÍF* II 1933, lix.

verið sögð. Þetta er bersýnilegt um konungasögur, þar sem vér sumsstaðar getum fylgt þroska hinna rituðu sagna stig af stigi. En sama máli gegnir um Íslendinga sögur, þótt með mismunandi hætti sé. Þær eru lika verk sagnaritara, höfunda, sem unnið hafa úr efninu og sett svip sinn á frásöguna.[3]

(... my own conclusion, after considering separate sagas and the development of saga-writing in general, is briefly this; that no saga now before us was written down in the form in which it was told. This is plainly true of the Kings' Sagas, where in some passages we can follow the development of the written text step by step. But the same rule applies to the Sagas of Icelanders, though in a different way. They too are the product of saga-writers, authors who have worked over the material and set their own stamp on the narrative.)

Nordal has this to say about the development of saga-writing in Iceland:

Í verkum Snorra nær sagnaritunin fyllsta samræmi vísinda og listar, skemmtilegrar frásagnar í taumhaldi sögulegrar dómgreindar. Hún hneigist enn meir í áttina til sögulegra skáldsagna, án þess að missa þó hinn raunverulega blæ, og nær þar nýju hámarki listarinnar í *Njálu*.[4]

(In the work of Snorri, saga-writing attains the fullest harmony of knowledge and art, attractive narrative controlled by historical judgement. The genre inclines ever more towards the historical novel, yet without sacrificing the touch of authenticity, and it was to reach a new pitch of artistry in *Njáls saga*.)

The basic principles here set out were to be further expressed in the introductions to other Sagas of Icelanders in *Íslenzk fornrit* during the following years and decades.[5] Nordal's essay "Hrafnkatla" was published in 1940, and there he argues that the principal events narrated in *Hrafnkels saga* never took place.[6] In this essay he also

---

3 Op. cit., lx.
4 Op. cit., lxiii.
5 See, for example, Einar Ól. Sveinsson in the introduction to *Laxdæla saga* (*ÍF* V, 1934) and to *Eyrbyggja saga* (*ÍF* IV, 1935). See further, Jón Jóhannesson, introduction to *Austfirðinga sögur* (*ÍF* XI, 1950).
6 Sigurður Nordal 1940, 66.

alludes to the objectives which had been followed in editing *Íslenzk fornrit*, and he says:

> Útgefendur *Fornritanna* hafa enn sem komið er yfirleitt gert of mikið úr þætti munnmælanna í efni Íslendinga sagna og hinu sögulega gildi þeirra. Höfundum sagnanna hefur ekki verið eignað meira en minnst varð komizt af með.[7]

(The editors of *Fornrit* texts up to now have, generally speaking, made too much of the element of oral tradition in the Sagas of Icelanders, and have over-estimated the historical value of such traditions. The authors of the sagas have been credited with no more than a grudging minimum.)

This passage sounds an express warning which needs to be kept in mind when estimating the material of the Sagas of Icelanders. But there has been a certain tendency in work on these sagas since 1940 to make generalizations from Nordal's essay on *Hrafnkels saga*;[8] for this reason it is as well to quote here some things he says in his conclusion:

> Þó að hér hafi ekki verið tóm til að gera samanburð á *Hrafnkötlu* og öðrum sögum, svo að neinu nemi, hefur verið reynt að láta það koma skýrt fram, að allar sögur mætti ekki mæla á einn kvarða, hvorki um sannindi, heimildir né efnismeðferð. Það er skoðun mín, sem ég hef fengið staðfesta hvað eftir annað, að hverja sögu beri að rannsaka sem gaumgæfilegast út af fyrir sig. Þótt þær heyri allar til einnar bókmenntagreinar og hin sameiginlegu einkenni liggi í augum uppi, skipta sérkenni hverrar sögu enn meira máli, bæði til þess að skilja hana sjálfa og til þess að fá yfirlit um þessa bókmenntagrein í heild og hverjum breytingum hún tók. Það væri jafnfráleitt, að ætla sér að kveða upp víðtæka dóma um sögurnar eftir athugun einnar þeirrar, eins og hitt, sem meir hefur brunnið við, að búa sér til almenna skoðun um þær og heimfæra hana síðan upp á hin ólíkustu verk.[9]

(Although I have not had space here to make any significant comparison between *Hrafnkels saga* and other sagas, I have tried to

---

7 Op. cit., 78.
8 Jónas Kristjánsson 1978, 304 ff. and Vésteinn Ólason 1983, 137 ff.
9 Sigurður Nordal 1940, 70.

make it plain that all sagas must not be measured by the same yardstick: not as to their veracity, nor their sources, nor their handling of material. In my opinion which I have been able to confirm time after time, every single saga should be most carefully analysed in its own right. Of course they all belong to one literary genre, and their common characteristics are immediately obvious. But the individuality of each separate saga is even more important: both to understand the work itself and also to achieve a general view of this type of literature as a whole, and to observe its variations. It would be altogether wide off the mark to propose sweeping judgements on sagas after considering one of them; and conversely, as has more often happened, to construct a generalized attitude to them and then impose it on the most diverse works.)

In 1953 Nordal published a chapter in *Nordisk kultur* on the Sagas of Icelanders. Here he divides the sagas into five groups, according to period of composition. Most of them (12 in all) fall into the second group, of which he says:

> Det maa antages, at alle sagaer i denne gruppe har et mere eller mindre betydeligt grundlag i *folkelig tradition.*[10]

> (It can be assumed that all the sagas in this group are to a more or less significant degree based on *popular tradition.*)

The same is of course even truer of the oldest sagas of all. The third group of sagas contains only five, including *Hrafnkels saga* and *Njáls saga.*[11]

I judged it necessary to make these points here about the "Icelandic School", and particularly about the work of Sigurður Nordal; for he was the originator of this school, he first blazed the trail, and he it was who took the main share in those studies that laid the foundations of the school.

The "Icelandic School" or the "Reykjavík School", as it was sometimes called, had an influence far beyond the borders of Iceland. Here I should like to refer to two scholars who were outstanding in the field about the middle of this century. Dag Strömbäck, in an article on the Sagas of Icelanders published in 1943, had this to say:

---

10 Sigurður Nordal 1953, 249.
11 Op. cit. , 235; 254.

De bygga i stor utsträckning på traditioner och muntliga berät-
telser, men i deras uppbyggnad och utgestaltning spåras namnlösa
diktare med snillets och inspirationens genius över sitt författar-
tarskap.[12]

(To a great extent they are based on traditions and oral narrative;
but their structure and formation bear the imprint of nameless
artists with a proper sense of the mastery and imagination of their
authorship.)

Ten years later, Gabriel Turville-Petre published *Origins of Icelandic Literature*, and he says this among other things about the
Sagas of Icelanders:

> The researches of recent years seem to suggest that the family sagas
> originated under the influence of the Kings' Sagas, just as the
> Kings' Sagas originated under the influence of hagiography and of
> other learned writing. This suggests that the family sagas were
> based on sources of many different kinds, on written records and
> genealogies, on the *Landnámabók,* works of Ari and other historical
> literature such as that discussed in earlier chapters of this book. It
> is widely agreed that the authors also used oral records, preserved
> both in prose and in verse.[13]

On the part played by authors in the writing of sagas, Turville-
Petre has this to say:

> Every family saga, if studied in detail, seems to bear the individual
> stamp of an author; it shows something of the author's personal
> interests and of his artistic taste.[14]

Much has been written on the Sagas of Icelanders in the last
three decades, and many theories have been put forward. In a recent
general survey, Jónas Kristjánsson gives an appraisal of these inves-
tigations, and he says:

> Í stað þess að líta á Íslendingasögur sem heimildir um söguöldina
> hafa menn í vaxandi mæli farið að líta á þær sem endurspeglun frá

---

12 Strömbäck 1970, 252.
13 Turville-Petre 1953, 231.
14 Op. cit, 233.

umhverfi höfundanna, íslenzku þjóðfélagi á þrettándu og fjórtándu öld. Sumir vilja hins vegar skoða þær sem skilgetið afkvæmi evrópskrar miðaldamenningar, jafnvel að þær séu ritaðar til að flytja ákveðnar kristilegar hugmyndir og siðaboð. Og loks koma svo bókmenntafræðingar og ritskýrendur sem vilja eingöngu meta sögurnar sem bókmenntaleg listaverk, með nokkurri gát á menningarstraumum ritunartímans.[15]

(Instead of regarding the Sagas of Icelanders as records of ancient Iceland, people have increasingly come to look on them as reflecting the environment of the authors, the Icelandic community in the thirteenth and fourteenth centuries. Some, on the other hand, would regard them as the true-born offspring of medieval European culture, would even suppose them written to convey definite Christian ideas and a moral message. And finally there come literary historians and critics whose one idea is to assess the sagas in terms of literary art, with some attention to cultural trends at the time of writing.)

Following up the words just quoted, Jónas Kristjánsson, gives his own estimate of the matter in hand:

Allir kunna þessir menn að hafa nokkuð til síns máls. En þeir sem líta á sögurnar einstrengingslega frá einhverju þessara sjónarmiða eru á villigötum, ekki síður en hinir sem trúa sögunum í blindni. Höfundar sagnanna vinna ekki sem frjálsir siðapredikarar eða listamenn. Þeir eru alltaf bundnir í annan skó af ætlunarverki sagnanna og af heimildum sínum: munnmælasögnum, vísum og kvæðum og eldri ritum.[16]

(There is something to be said for all of these views. But those who look at the sagas blinkered by any of these aspects are on the wrong track, no less than the others who hold a blind faith in the truth of the sagas. The authors were not acting as independent moralists or artists. They were always tied by the leg to the purpose of the stories and to their sources: oral traditions, verses and poems, and older works.)

The extracts I have quoted from criticism of the sagas in the last fifty years, together with references to some leading scholars of the

---

15 Jónas Kristjánson 1978, 272-273.
16 Op. cit., 273.

time, reveal an opinion once general and still dominant that Sagas of Icelanders are to some extent based on traditions. The next step is to consider whether there is any way of establishing the age of these traditions at the time when the authors of the sagas incorporated them. The Sagas of Icelanders for the most part tell of individuals living in the tenth and early eleventh centuries, reckoning by other historical sources. The question then arises whether records of these people survived in oral transmission all the time from the tenth century, or whether their names have been associated with traditions established later.

In folklore studies, it is a recognised fact that traditions are modified by the environment in which they survive. Traditions that migrate from one country to another change colour according to the area, and adjust themselves each time to the cultural environment in which they are recited.[17] On the other hand, traditions firmly formulated in one cultural environment can remain unchanged in new cultural surroundings for some time, long or short, even when they are at variance with current attitudes. Then it is their form that keeps them going.[18] We must always take these two contrasting principles of folklore study into account whenever we examine traditions that have travelled a long way in time or space.

The cultural environment in Iceland changed but little in the period between the completion of the settlement in the early tenth century and right up to the thirteenth century, when the Sagas of Icelanders were written. Domestic conditions would have been in the main exactly the same all this time, the size of the population was similar, habitation was just as scattered. The one change in this period that was of any significance and could have influenced the form and preservation of traditions was the Conversion (in A.D. 999 or 1000). The great majority of sagas deal with events which actually happened before the Conversion, some of them going back to the early tenth century. If traditions of leading characters had achieved a set form and stamp before A.D. 1000, they could perhaps still carry some trace over into the sagas. But then we have to reckon that these same traditions would have had to be orally preserved for

---

17 Anna Birgitta Rooth 1982, 140.
18 Op. cit., 141-142.

about two hundred years after the Conversion. Such transmission was likely to leave its mark, presumably as a tendency to discard ideas bearing the stamp of attitudes and concepts of Old Norse paganism. At the end of this process, in comes the author and adjusts the material to suit his story. Considering the progress of any conceivable traditions through nearly three centuries, not much of a harvest can be expected when we look for motifs of Old Norse paganism in the sagas.

Everywhere belief and religious practice are important elements in the creation of traditional stories. In the traditions of Christian communities, this feature usually takes the form of various powers, good or evil, which reward or punish the leading characters according to their deserts. By contrast, it is a usual feature of polytheistic religions for separate gods to take a hand in the course of affairs; they step out to defend their protégés and to oppose enemies of these. Here it is sufficient to refer to the poems of Homer, which produce too many examples of the Greek gods in this role for quotation here.[19] In the tenth century, when Old Norse paganism was dominant in Iceland, we may expect the Old Norse gods to resemble the Greek gods in this habit of meddling in the lives of their protégés, protecting or avenging them. Such intervention by the gods would most probably occur in stories of individual heroes circulating in the tenth century. Such traditions would inevitably fall on evil days after the Conversion, once the Old Norse gods had been uprooted from everyday experience. Of course it is true that the change of religion came about gradually and slowly, and even when the Old Norse gods had quitted the field various undergrowths of Old Norse belief remained in full vigour for a good while, becoming in course of time an active part of the superstition of the eleventh, twelfth and thirteenth centuries.[20] It is essential to allow for this alteration in traditional beliefs when we come to assess theological material in the Sagas of Icelanders.

Now I will set out some motifs in the sagas which could be taken as evidence of traditions formulated in the days of Norse

---

19 *Odysseifskviða* 1973, 293, 343, 351 and passim.
20 Strömbäck 1935, 3ff.; Jón Hnefill Aðalsteinsson 1978, 28-30 and references given there.

paganism. I have in my paper concentrated on motifs from two sagas, *Víga-Glúms saga* and *Gísla saga Súrssonar*.

In some passages of *Víga-Glúms saga* there are express references to the god Freyr. Early in the saga it is said that the temple of Freyr stood near the farm Þverá; and the property included the field *Vitazgjafi*, which never fell "barren".[21] Scholars have naturally assumed that Freyr was responsible for the fertility of the field, and thus it was consecrated to him, although this is not said outright.[22] When Sigmundr and Þorkell had unjustly appropriated the use of the field from Glúmr and his mother for a while, Glúmr killed Sigmundr on the spot. Glúmr won the case arising from the killing, and Þorkell had to hand over his part of Þverá. Then the saga says:

> Ok áðr Þorkell fór á brott frá Þverá, þá gekk hann til hofs Freys ok leiddi þagat uxa gamlan ok mælti svá: "Freyr," sagði hann, "er lengi hefir fulltrúi minn verit ok margar gjafar at mér þegit ok vel launat, nú gef ek þér uxa þenna til þess, at Glúmr fari eigi ónauðgari af Þverárlandi en ek fer nú. Ok láttu sjá nǫkkurar jartegnir, hvártú þiggr eða eigi." En uxanum brá svá við, at hann kvað við ok fell niðr dauðr, ok þótti Þorkatli vel hafa við látit ok var nú hughægra, er honum þótti sem þegit mundi heitit.[23]

> (Before Þorkell departed from Þverá, he went to the temple of Freyr, leading an old ox, and spoke thus: "Freyr," said he, "you who have long been the patron who has received many gifts from me and repaid them well, I now give you this ox, in order that Glúmr may leave Þverárland under no less compulsion than I do now. Manifest some signs to show whether you accept or not." The effect on the ox was such that it bellowed and fell dead; and Þorkell thought the answer favourable, and was now easier in mind, when it seemed to him that the prayer had been heard.)

The next allusion to Freyr is in connection with the outlawry of Vigfúss, son of Víga-Glúmr. Of him it is said:

En hann mátti eigi heima vera fyrir helgi staðarins ok helt Glúmr

---

21 *ÍF* IX 1956, 16, 22.
22 Op. cit., 22 n. 1 and works cited there.
23 Op. cit., 34.

hann á laun. En því skyldu eigi sekir menn þar vera, at Freyr leyfði eigi, er hof þat átti, er þar var.[24]

(But he could not live at home because of the consecration of the place; and Glúmr kept him in hiding. And men under penalty were not admitted because Freyr, deity of the temple there, did not allow it.)

Freyr last appears in the saga when enemies of Víga-Glúmr once more bring a case of homicide against him, a case that ends with Glúmr being forced to give up Þverá and leave. The saga says:

En áðr Glúmr riði heiman, dreymði hann, at margir menn væri komnir þar til Þverár at hitta Frey, ok þóttisk hann sjá mart manna á eyrunum við ána, en Freyr sat á stóli. Hann þóttisk spyrja, hverir þar væri komnir. Þeir svara: "Þetta eru frændr þínir framliðnir, ok biðjum vér nú Frey, at þú sér eigi á brott færðr af Þverárlandi, ok tjóar ekki, ok svarar Freyr stutt ok reiðuliga ok minnisk nú á uxagjǫf Þorkels ins háva". Hann vaknaði, ok lézk Glúmr verr vera við Frey alla tíma síðan.[25]

(Before Glúmr rode away from home, he dreamt that many people had come to Þverá to meet Freyr, and he seemed to see a crowd on the gravel banks by the river, while Freyr sat on a throne. He thought he asked who they were. They answered: "These are your departed kinsmen, and we are praying to Freyr that you should not be taken away from Þverárland; but all in vain, for Freyr answers shortly and angrily, and he remembers the gift of an ox by Þorkell the Tall". He awoke, and Glúmr said his relations with Freyr were worse ever after.)

Now we must explain the connection between the cult of Freyr and Glúmr's occupation of Þverá. A diagram will show it thus:

Cult of Freyr	*Activities of Glúmr*	*Activities of Glúmr's enemies*
Freyr's temple Vitazgjafi Legal sanction on Þverá	Killing of Sigmundr Presence of Vigfúss under penalty	Þorkell the Tall gives an ox

24 Op. cit., 66.
25 Op. cit., 87-88.

All three activities here shown point directly to the destruction of Glúmr's right to live at Þverá. Indeed it appears that in the days of active paganism in Iceland the dedication of an ox by Þorkell the Tall would alone have been enough to get Glúmr out of Þverá. We have only to take account of the portents accompanying the gift, and also to notice Freyr's subsequent answer, revealed to Glúmr in dream according to the saga. Sacrilege in the field was also bound to do Glúmr great damage, according to the concepts of Old Norse paganism. In terms of the general religious outlook, it was a case of grave and gross sacrilege, not likely to be left unavenged by the gods. The third point, the sanctity imposed on Þverá by Freyr and the god's prohibition of the presence of men under penalty, is especially interesting from the point of view of theology and administration. The motif here expressed, indistinct and laconic though it is, turns our thoughts to the links between administration and pagan worship in tenth-century Iceland, a matter that has been much discussed. Elsewhere I have given rather full attention to these links, and to the role of the *goðar* and their activity in this area; so I refer you to this work.[26] But the isolated motif shown here gives valuable support to conclusions already reached by other means: that a close and unbroken link existed between cult and administration in tenth-century Iceland.

I have just glanced at the accounts of Freyr in *Víga-Glúms saga* in the light of Old Norse beliefs. If these beliefs are regarded as a living religion, and the god Freyr as an active object of worship, then these traditions preserve memories of forces which could well be the basis and explanation of a momentous result. There is an obvious logic in this account of Freyr, and it is easy to perceive the causes and effects which set a story or tradition on its way.

The next step is to consider the place of these traditions of Freyr in *Víga-Glúms saga* itself, and what part they play in the development of the story. The short answer is that these passages make little difference to the development, and nowhere count as a motive force in the plot. When Glúmr kills Sigmundr in the field Vitazgjafi, it is simply stated as a fact, and the mention of Þorkell the Tall sacrificing an ox is entirely neutral. The same is true of the pas-

---

26 *Blót* and *Þing*, pp. 35-56 above.

sage where Víga-Glúmr pollutes Þverá by secretly sheltering his outlawed son. No particular results of this deed come into the story. Towards the end of the saga it is finally mentioned that Víga-Glúmr dreamed of Freyr, just before the prosecution was brought up at the Assembly which closed with his expulsion from Þverá. The fact that Freyr in a dream forbids Glúmr to live at Þverá any longer is treated casually. Other points are brought up, which are considered more relevant to the expulsion of Glúmr from Þverá and his final downfall.

Thus Freyr is not really operative in *Víga-Glúms saga*, and his divinity has no motive power in the story. But other, more potent incidents do occur. First of all, there are the treasures given to Víga-Glúmr by his maternal grandfather, Vigfúss of Vors:

> ... einkagripi vil ek þér gefa, feld ok spjót ok sverð, er vér hǫfum mikinn trúnað á haft frændr; ok meðan þú átt gripina, vænti ek, at þú týnir eigi virðingu, en þá em ek hræddr um, ef þú lógar þeim.[27]

> (... and I will give you especial treasures, a cloak, a spear and a sword, in which all our kin has put great faith; as long as you keep possession of these treasures, I do not expect you to lose your distinction; but I fear for it, if you part with them.)

Then there is the occasion when Glúmr dreams of a stately woman whom he invites to his home. His interpretation of the dream is that the guardian-spirit of his grandfather, recently dead, is seeking out an abode.[28] Soon after, it is stated:

> Glúmr tók nú virðing mikla í heraðinu.[29]

> (Glúmr now gained a high reputation in that district.)

The plain inference is that the good-fortune of his grandfather had a favourable effect. The auspicious treasures of Vigfús come into the story again, when Einar of Þverá says:

---

27 *ÍF* IX 1956, 19.
28 Op. cit., 30-31.
29 Op. cit., 35.

Glúmr hefir nú lógat þeim hlutum, feldi ok spjóti, er Vigfúss, móðurfaðir hans, gaf honum ok bað hann eiga, ef hann vildi halda virðingu sinni, en kvað þaðan frá þverra mundu. Nú mun ek taka við málinu ok fylgja.[30]

(Glúm has now parted with the cloak and spear that Vigfús his grandfather gave him, enjoining him to keep them if he wanted to retain his reputation; but he said it would be on the wane thenceforth. Now is the time for me to take up the prosecution, and press it.)

Predictably, Glúmr lost the case, but he was still reluctant to leave Þverá, and sat himself in the place of honour at the time when he had to depart. Then came Hallbera, mother of Einar, the new master of Þverá, and addressed him in these words:

... komit hefi ek nú eldi á Þverárland, ok geri ek þik nú á brott með allt þitt, ok er helgat landit Einari, syni mínum.[31]

(I have now taken fire to Þverárland, and I expel you and all yours, and the land is appropriated to my son Einar.)

At this juncture, Glúmr could in no way keep his position, and he took himself off from Þverá.

It is instructive to compare the references to Freyr with those events here mentioned, which are in truth the motive force of the story. I shall turn first to a theological equation, which would have held good in the tenth century, when Old Norse paganism was in force in Iceland. In those days we can expect to find a belief in personified fate, such as the figure Glúmr is said to have dreamt. It may also be reckoned that various things were considered lucky objects, connected with some kind of belief. It is also plain in various Old Icelandic sources that in pagan times it was an active and well-known custom to take possession of land by carrying fire round it. Yet this practice applied exclusively to land not already belonging to other people; for the person who carried fire round took possession of the land by this means, according to the laws of gods and

---

30 Op. cit., 87.
31 Op. cit., 89.

men.[32] It will be clear that the above-mentioned beliefs were in the tenth century assigned a level lower than belief in the Old Norse gods themselves. Personal luck, lucky objects, and rites of possession in taking land must all have been subordinate to the gods worshipped, those who controlled the fates of men and things yet to come, who ruled over the winds and weather, and the fertility of man and beast.[33]

The Conversion brought a total change of this conceptual system. The Old Norse gods vanished from the scene, but many other products of Old Norse belief continued to thrive, and turned into *superstition* as it was called, as soon as the one true religion had entered the country. The way *Víga-Glúms saga* uses the practice of encircling land with fire is especially arresting. This custom, which had been a legal method of taking possession, one of the links between religion and law, becomes in this narrative a kind of aversion-charm, the cunning contrivance of an old woman safeguarding the interests of her son.[34] It is a frequent feature of religious history that various practices of an older religion will, under the new dispensation, become means of sorcery. This is what might have happened here.[35]

In view of these matters, it is natural that mention of the god Freyr falls into the background in *Víga-Glúms saga*, and exercises no motive power in the development of the story. Instances of superstition accord better with the range of ideas in the eleventh, twelfth and thirteenth centuries, and with the state of things confronting people at that time. The fact that traditions of Freyr are nevertheless preserved in *Víga-Glúms saga* strongly suggests to me that they had at some time played an effective part in traditions about Víga-Glúmr. The inner logic of these accounts, where the result follows on from the cause, can most plausibly be traced to the tenth century, when the Old Norse religion was a living force and Freyr was actively worshipped. This, it seems to me, is a basis for

---

32 Strömbäck 1970, 135 ff.
33 See Snorri Sturluson, *Edda* 1931, 31 ff., 41.
34 Cf. Strömbäck 1970, 150 f. and references where slightly different view is expressed.
35 Jón Hnefill Aðalsteinsson 1978, 21 and works cited there.

dating the initial formation of traditions in the Sagas of Icelanders all the way back to the tenth century. It is harder to establish just when Freyr gave way before the instances of superstition, but I would think that this happened at least to some extent while traditions about Glúmr were circulating orally. All the same, it can never be firmly decided what changes occurred in oral tradition, or what was thereafter the work of the author of *Víga-Glúms saga*.

There are some references to Freyr in the saga of Gísli Súrsson. It is said of the chieftain Þorgrímr Þorsteinsson, also called "Freysgoði" (priest of Freyr):

> Þorgrímr ætlaði at hafa haustboð at vetrnóttum ok fagna vetri ok blóta Frey ok býðr þangat Berki bróðr sínum ok Eyjólfi Þórðar syni ok mǫrgu ǫðru stórmenni.[36]

> (Þorgrímr planned to hold an autumn feast at the time of the Winter Nights to welcome winter and sacrifice to Freyr; he invited his brother Bǫrkr and Eyjólfr Þórðarson, and many other leading men.)

The night after the feast, Gísli Súrsson got secretly into the sleeping-hall of the farm at Sæból, as in this description:

> Nú gengr hann innar eptir húsinu ok at lokhvílunni, þar er þau Þorgrímr hvíldu ok systir hans, ok var hnigin hurð á gátt, ok eru þau bæði í rekkju. Gengr hann þangat ok þreifask fyrir ok tekr á brjósti henni, ok hvíldi hon nær stokki. Síðan mælti hon Þórdís: "Hví er svá kǫld hǫnd þín, Þorgrímr?" ok vekr hann. Þorgrímr mælti: "Viltu at ek snúumk at þér?" Hon hugði, at hann legði hǫndina yfir hana. Gísli bíðr þá enn um stund ok vermir hǫndina í serk sér, en þau sofna bæði. Nú tekr hann á Þorgrími kyrrt, svá at hann vaknaði. Hann hugði, at hon Þórdís vekði hann, ok snerisk þá at henni. Gísli tekr þá klæðin af þeim annarri hendi, en með annarri leggr hann í gegnum Þorgrím með Grásíðu, svá at í beðinum nam stað.[37]

> (He moved to the inside of the building and to the bed-closet where his sister and Þorgrímr were sleeping; the door was closed, and both were in bed. He went up, feeling his way, and touched

---

36 *ÍF* VI 1943, 50. See further *Blót* and *Þing* above, p. 41.
37 Op. cit., 53-54.

the woman's breast, for she was lying next the bed-board. Then said Þórdís, "Why is your hand so cold, Þorgrímr?" and woke him. Þorgrímr said, "Do you want me to turn towards you?" She had supposed that it was Þorgrímr putting his arm across her. Gísli waited for some time, and warmed his hand in his bosom, and they both fell asleep. Now he touched Þorgrímr lightly, enough to wake him. Þorgrímr supposed that Þórdís had woken him, and turned towards her. Gísli then stripped the bedclothes from them with one hand, and with the other he stabbed Þorgrímr with the spear Grásíða, so that it stuck in the slats under the bedding.)

Gísli escaped, and no-one knew who did the killing. He helped to bury Þorgrímr. Soon after, the saga says:

> Varð ok sá hlutr einn, er nýnæmum þótti gegna, at aldri festi snæ útan ok sunnan á haugi Þorgríms ok eigi fraus; ok gátu menn þess til, at hann myndi Frey svá ávarðr fyrir blótin, at hann myndi eigi vilja, at frøri á milli þeira.[38]

> (Now a certain thing felt to be unprecedented was that snow never lay on the seaward and southern side of Þorgrímr's mound, and there was no frost; and people concluded that he must be so dear to Freyr because of the sacrifices he had offered, that the god would not tolerate any chill between them.)

Then we are told that the same winter people were holding ball-games, when the bat cracked, and Gísli offered to repair it:

> Gísli sezk niðr ok gerir at trénu, horfir á hauginn Þorgríms; snær var á jǫrðu, en konur sátu upp í brekkuna, Þórdís systir hans ok margar aðrar. Gísli kvað þá vísu,[39]

> (Gísli sat down to mend the bat, looking towards Þorgrímr's mound. There was snow on the ground, and the women were sitting on the bank above, Gísli's sister Þórdís and many others. Gísli then spoke a verse.)

In this verse, Gísli let out that he had killed Þorgrímr. His sister Þórdís, widow of Þorgrímr, memorised the verse and then "worked

---

38 Op. cit., 57.
39 Op. cit., 58.

it out", that is, she grasped the full sense of what it meant. From that moment, Gísli's fate was sealed.

I will now consider the probable age of the passages I have quoted, with some attention to any inner cohesion there may be between them. The account of Þorgrímr's autumn sacrifice is short and factual, and offers no particular information about the method or practice of sacrifice. Such general description as it contains could be widely available to the author of the saga. The description of how Gísli went to the sleeping-place of Þorgrímr and Þórdís at night after the sacrifice is altogether more copious and precise. There is a parallel to this account in *Droplaugarsona saga*, in the passage where Grímr Droplaugarson kills Helgi Ásbjarnarson at Eiðar. This is how it goes:

Þá gekk Grímr í hvílugólf þat, er var hjá sæng þeira Helga, ok setti þar niðr fyrir framan þat, er hann hafði í hendi, ok gekk síðan at sænginni ok lagði af Helga klæðin. Hann vaknaði við ok mælti: "Tóktu á mér, Þórdís, eða hví var svá kǫld hǫnd þín?" "Eigi tók ek á þér," sagði hon, "ok óvarr ert þú. Uggir mik, at til mikils dragi um." Ok eptir þat sofnuðu þau. Þá gekk Grímr at Helga ok tók hǫnd Þórdísar af honum, er hon hafði lagt yfir hann. Grímr mælti: "Vaki þú, Helgi, fullsofit er." En síðan lagði Grímr sverðinu á Helga, svá at stóð í gegnum hann.[40]

(Then Grímr went into the closet enclosing the bed of Helgi and Þórdís, setting down in front of it what he was carrying [i.e. the small round stick]. Next he went to the bed and turned the bed-clothes off Helgi. He woke at this, and said, "Did you touch me, Þórdís, and why was your hand so cold?" "I didn't touch you," said she, "and you are reckless. I fear that great trouble is on the way." And after that they fell asleep. Grímr then went to Helgi and lifted off the arm that Þórdís had thrown over him. Grímr said, "Wake up, Helgi, you have slept long enough." And then Grímr struck Helgi with the sword and ran him through.)

Scholars soon noticed the similarity of these two accounts, but have not agreed on which of the two has drawn on the other.[41] Jón Jóhannesson alludes to these researches in his introduction to *Aust-*

---

40 *ÍF* XI 1950, 170.
41 Björn K. Þórólfsson in *ÍF* VI 1943, xx n. 1 and works cited there.

firðinga sögur in *Íslenzk fornrit:* "Hugðu menn lengi að *Droplaugarsona saga* væri þiggjandinn, en síðustu rannsóknir hafa leitt hið gagn-stæða í ljós, svo að eigi verður um villzt, enda styður *Íslendingadrápa* kjarnann í frásögn hennar."[42] (For a long time, *Droplaugarsona saga* was taken to be the borrower, but most recent researches have demonstrated the opposite; there can be no doubt about it, for the poem *Íslendinga drápa* supports the nucleus of the saga account.) The researches that Jón Jóhannesson refers to are found in the introduction to the edition of *Gísla saga* by Björn K. Þórólfsson in *Íslenzk fornrit*. This editor compares the two accounts, and finds two decisive points to show that *Gísla saga* is here drawing on *Droplaugarsona saga*. One concerns the clothing of the assassin, the other the relative positions of sleeping-hall and byre in the farms Sæból and Eiðar; and further, the purpose of tying together the cows' tails in the byre in each context. Björn K. Þórólfsson says that on both these points the account of *Droplaugarsona saga* is consistent, while that of *Gísla saga* is inconsistent and redundant.[43] This is true enough, yet these two points do not seem to me as weighty or decisive as Björn and Jón think. What matters most, it seems to me, is that these scholars have not made a detailed comparison in those sections that are after all most important in each separate account; namely, the description of the killing. I will now take these sections, referring to the passages I have already quoted.

The account of *Gísla saga* has one feature over and above that of *Droplaugarsona saga*, when it tells of the talk and mutual relations of Þorgrímr and Þórdís in bed. "Do you want me to turn towards you?" says Þorgrímr when he wakes for the first time. The sense of this question is clear, for it means straightforwardly "Do you want me to have intercourse with you?" When again a few lines further on it is said that Þorgrímr "thought that it was Þórdís waking him, and he then turned towards her," the meaning is equally clear. Þorgrímr turns to his wife to have intercourse with her, and at the same instant he is stabbed to death.

This feature has no parallel in other sagas, and therefore it seems natural to suppose that here we have the residue of a tradition about

---

42 *ÍF* XI 1950, lxxiii.
43 *ÍF* VI 1943, xix-xx and works cited there.

the slaying of Þorgrímr. The next task is to consider whether this episode could have had any particular significance at any time in the period when the tradition would have arisen, roughly speaking between the years 960 and 1240.

In terms of Christian thought, there is no particular significance in a man being killed in the circumstances described, except in so far as the tragedy is made unusually gruesome. It becomes a totally different matter if this account is set in the conceptual and theological context of the tenth century.

In fertility cults, ritual worship or celebration culminates with the king/ high priest or the god of sacrifice copulating with the appropriate consort.[44] In this way he brings the rite to an end; and we may think that Þorgrímr, the 25-year old priest of Freyr, was playing this role when he is made to say to his wife Þórdís: "Do you want me to turn towards you?" And so, when soon after he turns to his wife to have intercourse with her, and is stabbed to death in the act, it is not simply a matter of a man being killed in his bed at night; it is rather that the presiding priest is killed while completing the ritual. By tenth-century standards, the death of Þorgrímr would have been not simply murder by night, but also sacrilege of the gravest kind.

Freyr was god of fertility and fruitfulness in general, of the fertility of men and beasts in particular. The poem *Skírnismál* depicts his impatient longing for his own marriage; Adam of Bremen says that the idol of Freyr in the temple at Uppsala was carved with a gigantic priapus; and an image found in Sweden which is generally thought to represent Freyr has the same distinctive feature.[45] Considering all this, I regard it as no accident that a text which records the killing of Þorgrímr should take special trouble to demonstrate that at the point of death Þorgrímr was exactly like Freyr.

Þorgrímr was killed about forty years before the Conversion. Thus there was plenty of opportunity for a tradition of the slaying to be fully formulated and established while the Old Norse religion was still dominant in the country. At that time, all the circum-

---

44 David 1980, 103; Eliade 1983, 331-366 and references.
45 *Sæmundar-Edda. Eddukvæði* 1926, 83-84; Adam of Bremen 1917, 257; and Turville-Petre 1964, 248 n. 51.

stances would be seen from the standpoint of Old Norse belief; cause and effect would be interpreted in accordance with current concepts. It seems to me that these concepts and this interpretation can still be read between the lines of *Gísla saga*, once it is carefully examined. As far as transmission of the episode goes, we can call to mind that Snorri *goði* was present in bed with his parents, as yet unborn. Snorri became the father of Þuríðr, the wise, well-informed and reliable woman who supplied material to Ari *fróði*. So in this case there were unusually fair prospects that a tradition would be kept alive over a long period, undamaged and word-for-word as it had originally been formulated.

A priest of Freyr who was killed in the fertility episode of ritual had reason to expect a special reward from the god of fertility. According to *Gísla saga*, Þorgrímr did not have long to wait for the recompense. A "thing without precedent" happened: his mound stayed unfrozen, and people assumed that Freyr would not tolerate any frosty relations between them. This "unprecedented thing" brought about the fall of Þorgrímr's slayer. Gísli lost sight of his own interests as he looked at the mound, and composed a verse which gave him away.

The theological chain of reasoning in the situation I have described is quite clear. It seems to me so clear and logical that it is hard to entertain any other idea than that it was formulated in the days of Old Norse paganism, while Freyr was still a powerful and living pagan god.

In *Gísla saga*, little weight is given to the traditions of Freyr here recounted. Their function in the narrative is more or less a form of in-filling, and they are not regarded as making any difference to the development of events. The saga puts it in this way, when Þorgrímr has been buried:

> ... Bǫrkr kaupir at Þorgrími nef, at hann seiddi seið, at þeim manni yrði ekki at bjǫrg, er Þorgrím hefði vegit.[46]

> (... Bǫrkr struck an agreement with Þorgrímr "the Claw", who was to bring it about by shamanistic practices that the man who had slain Þorgrímr should be deprived of all succour.)

---

46 *ÍF* VI 1956, 56.

The shamanism of Þorgrímr the Claw is described immediately before the mention of the "unprecedented thing" at the mound of Þorgrímr, priest of Freyr, and in such a way as to give readers the impression that Gísli composes the verse under the influence of the spell. The methods used by this Þorgrímr are described in a very general way.

Shamanistic practices survived the Conversion, but black magic and incantations were forbidden.[47] Another item from the realm of Christian superstition which is influential in *Gísla saga* is the ill-fated weapon Grásíða.[48] These manifestations of superstition were no doubt in full vigour in the first centuries after the Conversion, right up to the author's own time. The practices in question are similar to those already discussed in connection with *Víga-Glúms saga*. Superstitious practices are allowed to operate as a motive force in the story, while a traditional pattern associated with the god Freyr lies in the background, inactive for the most part. We may think that this traditional pattern was formulated in the days of Old Norse paganism, when Freyr was still a potent and living god.

Translated by Joan Turville-Petre

---

47 Strömbäck 1935, 61 ff.
48 *ÍF* VI 1956, 5, 6, 9, 12, 13, 37, 52, and 54.

*This paper was read at the University of Oxford on November 18 1985, and originally published in *Gripla* VII 1990.

POSTSCRIPT

SACRILEGE IN A MARITAL BED was presented in the form of a lecture at Oxford University in November 1985 under the title of OLD NORSE RELIGION IN THE SAGAS OF ICELANDERS, and accepted for publishing in *Gripla* early in 1986. The publication was delayed and the paper did not appear until 1990. Two years later, I took up the main points concerning the account of the slaying of Þorgrímr the *goði* in an article called "Freysminni í fornsögum" ("Freyr Motifs in the Sagas") which appeared in *Íslensk félagsrit*.[49]

The events in the bed-closet when Gísli killed Þorgrímr have been taken up in several articles since 1985. In 1986, an article appeared by Preben Meulengracht-Sørensen entitled "Murder in marital bed. An attempt at understanding a crucial scene in *Gísla saga*". Meulengracht-Sørensen discusses in particular the description of Gísli before he kills Þorgrímr. He notes the explanations given by other scholars, as well as some interesting comparative material.[50] His discussion therefore has a slightly different basis from mine, and only indirectly comes into contact with the main logic behind my argument, which is related to the description of the events in the bed-closet itself, and the account concerning Þorgrímr's green mound.

Guðrún Nordal touches on the same material in her article, "Freyr fífldur" ("Freyr cheated") which appeared in 1992, and follows my interpretation of the events without comment.[51]

In his article "Morð í rekkju hjóna" ("Murder in a marital bed") from 1994, Vésteinn Ólason takes up the same question. He discusses it along similar lines to those taken by Meulengracht-Sørensen, emphasising the artistic and aesthetic qualities of the narrative. Vésteinn takes up my suggestion that the extant account of the events and the conversation in the bed-closet might be based on an oral tradition, and says:

> Þessi túlkun er ekki í neinni mótsögn við þá skýringu sem hér hefur verið gefin á hátterni Gísla en eykur við frásögnina nýrri vídd og fellir atburðina í nýtt munstur þar sem verk Gísla er skilið sem brot gegn Frey sem síðan stuðlar að refsingu hans.[52]

---

49 Jón Hnefill Aðalsteinsson, in *Íslensk félagsrit* 1990-1992, 72-76.
50 Meulengracht-Sørensen 1986, 247-258.
51 Guðrún Nordal 1992, 285.
52 Vésteinn Ólason 1994, 827-828.

(This interpretation in no way opposes the explanation that has been given here regarding Gísli's behaviour, but adds another dimension to the account, placing the events in a new pattern in which Gísli's actions are taken as being a crime against Freyr which helps lead towards his eventual punishment.)

Preben Meulengracht-Sørensen, Guðrún Nordal and Vésteinn Ólason have all correctly drawn attention to the obvious references in the account of Þorgrímr's murder to the description of the murder of Sigurðr Fáfnisbani given in the poem *Sigurðarkviða in skamma*.[53] The strophe in question (st. 24) runs as follows:

Sofnuð var Guðrún	Guðrún was asleep
í sæingu	in bed
sorgalaus	with no cares
hjá Sigurði;	beside Sigurðr;
enn hón vaknaði	but she awoke
vilja firð,	removed from joy,
er hón Freys vinar	she was floating
flaut í dreyra.[54]	in the blood of the friend of Freyr.

To my mind, the references to *Sigurðarkviða in skamma* and to Sigurðr himself as "the friend of Freyr" support the religious interpretation I pose in my article about the direct relationship between the conversation of Þorgrímr and Þórdís in the bed-closet, and the fertility of Þorgrímr's grave mound which Freyr shielded throughout the winter.

The intrinsic connection between the motif of the sacrilege in the marital bed and that of the fertility of the grass which grew on Þorgrímr's grave mound in wintertime nonetheless rules out the idea that the account in *Gísla saga Súrssonar* should originally stem from *Sigurðarkviða in skamma*.

---

53 Meulengracht-Sørensen 1986, 253; Guðrún Nordal 1992, 285-286, and Vésteinn Ólason 1994, 826.
54 *Sæmundaredda. Eddukvæði* 1926, 338.

Ágrip

Helgispjöll í hjónarekkju

Í SLENDINGASÖGUR eru torræðar og vandmeðfarnar heimildir um norræna trú. Því ber nauðsyn til, áður en litið er á slík dæmi í sögunum, að hyggja að rannsóknarsögu síðustu áratuga og líta á niðurstöður fremstu vísindamanna um hvernig Íslendingasögur séu til orðnar. Fyrir þá rannsókn sem hér er gerð skiptir mestu máli hvort gera megi ráð fyrir gömlum sagnleifum í sögunum sem hugsanlega væru frá dögum norrænnar trúar.

Í formála *Egils sögu* árið 1933, sem var stefnumótandi fyrir viðhorf útgefenda *Íslenzkra fornrita*, segir Sigurður Nordal, að meginefni margra Íslendingasagna sé sótt í munnlegar frásögur, en sögurnar séu verk höfunda sem hafi farið frjálslega með efni sitt. Í verkum Snorra Sturlusonar nái sagnaritunin fyllstu samræmi vísinda og listar. Sama grundvallarviðhorf til Íslendingasagna setti Sigurður Nordal einnig fram í *Nordisk kultur* tuttugu árum síðar. Þar segir hann, að meginhluti Íslendingasagna byggi að meira eða minna leyti á arfsögnum. Meira vafamál telur hann um arfsagnirnar hvað sumar yngri sögurnar varðar, en í þeim hópi eru *Hrafnkels saga* og *Njáls saga*. Í ritgerð um Hrafnkels sögu hafði Sigurður Nordal einnig varað við því að heimfæra þær niðurstöður sem hann komst þar að á önnur verk.

Sigurður Nordal var frumkvöðull og brautryðjandi hins svonefnda „Íslenska skóla", sem kom fram sem arftaki „bókfestu-" og „sagnfestukenninga", og var mikils ráðandi um miðja öldina og gætir allt fram á þennan dag. Af talsmönnum þess skóla utan Íslands má sérstaklega nefna Dag Strömbäck og Gabriel Turville-Petre. Í nýlegu yfirlitsriti um Íslendingasögur heldur Jónas Kristjánsson fram svipuðum viðhorfum og hér hafa verið rakin. Hann gerir grein fyrir kenningum um Íslendingasögur er fram hafa komið á síðustu áratugum og telur höfunda þeirra alla kunna að hafa nokkuð til síns máls. En hann bætir við, að einstrengingsleg fastheldni við einstakar kenningar leiði menn á villigötur, því að höfundar Íslendingasagna séu bundnir í annan skó af ætlunarverki sagnanna og heimildum sínum, sögnum, bundnu máli og eldri ritum.

Torvelt er að færa rök að hugsanlegum aldri munnmælasagna í Íslendingasögum. Þau tímamörk sem helst verður tekið mið af eru kristnitakan. Þá vaknar sú spurning, hvort unnt sé að leiða líkur að því, að enn megi finna í sögunum sagnamunstur er beri þess einkenni að hafa orðið til fyrir kristnitöku.

Í *Víga-Glúms sögu* eru nokkrar frásagnir um samskipti Víga-Glúms og Freys. Víga-Glúmur vanhelgar það sem guðinum tilheyrir og guðinum er færð fórn til að koma Víga-Glúmi frá Þverá. Niðurstaðan verður sú, að Víga-Glúmur verður að láta jörðina af hendi. Hér er til staðar innra samhengi orsaka og afleiðinga sem gæti borið vitni viðhorfum tíundu aldar. Í Víga-Glúms sögu eru þessi minni þó óvirk og þar eru ýmis atriði úr hjátrú elleftu, tólftu og þrettándu aldar látin fleyta fram atburðarás. Sú staðreynd, að heillegt sagnamunstur úr hugarheimi norrænnar trúar er þrátt fyrir allt enn í sögunni, er veigamikil röksemd fyrir því, að umræddar sagnir hafi mótast meðan norræn trú var enn ríkjandi á Íslandi.

Í *Gísla sögu Súrssonar* segir frá Freysdýrkun Þorgríms, sem Gísli Súrsson vó í hjónarekkjunni við lok haustblóts. Frásögn sögunnar dregur fram, að Þorgrímur hafi engum verið líkari en Frey á banastundinni. Haugur Þorgríms hélst þíður og var þakkað Frey. Gísli leit til haugsins og kvað vísu þar sem hann lýsti sig banamann Þorgríms. Hér virðist auðlesið trúarsögulegt samhengi helgispjalla í hjónarekkjunni og gróðurnála sem uxu á haugi Þorgríms að vetri til. Þessir atburðir gegna þó ekki samfelldu hlutverki í sögunni, þar sem atburðarás er borin uppi af ýmsum hjátrúarfyrirbærum. Hér er hins vegar að öllum líkindum um sagnleif frá tíundu öld að ræða, er tekið hafði á sig mynd meðan Freyr var enn lifandi og virkur guð.

Myth and Ritual in Glúma *and* Hrafnkatla

THE ICELANDIC FAMILY SAGAS have for a long time held a place of permanent value in world literature and in this capacity they are read and studied in the universities of many countries. All the same, I think it proper at the beginning of this lecture to say a few words about their origin and the cultural environment from which they sprang. I also want here at the start to make special mention of possible traces of Old Norse mythology and Old Norse pagan faith which may exist in the sagas and consider the most appropriate means of demonstrating that traces of this sort do exist. The Family Sagas were written down in the thirteenth century but they tell of people who would have lived in the tenth and eleventh centuries, of their lives and their fortunes. Scholars in this field are now agreed, almost without exception, that the sagas are the work of individual authors, each saga bearing the imprint of its writer. On the other hand, there is still discussion as to what sources were of prime importance to each author, and also whether authors drew more on material from the literature of Europe in general, or from the traditions which were arguably current in Iceland itself. This discussion has a direct bearing on the material I am handling here. The Conversion took place in Iceland round about the turn of the year one 1000. Up till then, Old Norse paganism had prevailed almost unchallenged for a good hundred years, but now it receded, bit by bit and more or less imperceptably. When we turn our attention to traces of Old Norse mythology and Old Norse beliefs in the sagas, we should expect results principally in traditions that took shape and form as early as the tenth century. Tradition was therefore orally transmitted with little or no alteration until the authors of the sagas incorporated it in their own works. Granted these conditions, we can, of course not expect to find many actual messages in the Icelandic sagas, that is narratives about the Old Norse gods in person, accounts which the earliest reciters held to be both true and sacred.

When I use the term "myth", I am referring to accounts of the usual connotation, narratives concerning divine or supernatural beings.

This entails just about the same expression of the concept as that current among anthropologists and theologians who have concentrated their researches upon previously little-known myths of people scattered across the world, and all this during the last hundred years.[1] There is no reason to think that parallel myths were not also current in Iceland in the tenth century. Myths treating the Old Norse gods and their relations to humankind from the point of view of people who believed in the Old Norse gods were both sacred and true and it was incumbent on everyone to model his life and behaviour in conformity with them. From the point of view of the Christian authors of the sagas, such tales were both untrue and ridiculous. It is appropriate to glance at the opinions of scholars on possible conditions present in the Icelandic sagas. Sigurður Nordal, in a book published in 1942, wrote of the Icelandic sagas as sources of cultural history:

> Þó að Íslendinga sögur séu mörgu blandnar, óáreiðanlegum sögnum, áhrifum úr samtíðinni, skáldskap, viðleitni að glæsa fortíðina, eru þær ekki lítils verðar. Þar er ýmis fróðleikur um atburði, sem gerzt hafa í raun og veru, þótt mörgu skakki um atvik og lýsingar. Aðrar eins bókmenntir, jafnþjóðlegar, sjálfstæðar og sérstæðar, þrátt fyrir erlend áhrif, spretta ekki upp úr óræktaðri jörð. Enginn yrkir út yfir vébönd þess, sem hann getur hugsað eða hefur þroska til. Sögurnar eiga sér rætur í menningu þeirrar aldar, sem þær segja frá, og það skiptir hér mestu.[2]

> (Although the Family Sagas contained many and varied strands, unreliable traditions, contemporary impulses, fiction, attempts to glamorise the past, they are not valueless as they contain much information about events that actually happened, although there may be much amiss in detail and interpretation. Cultures of this sort, so native, independent and eccentric in defiance of outside influences, these do not spring from untilled soil. No one can carry on husbandry of this kind beyond the limits of imagination and his capacity. The sagas have their roots in the culture of the period they are telling of, and that is what counts for most in this case.)

Nordal's conclusion that the Family Sagas are rooted in the cul-

---

1 Eliade 1973, 306-318. Cf. Lindow 1985, 21ff.
2 Sigurður Nordal 1942, 135.

ture of the period they tell of serves as the foundation of the present discussion. It would be possible to cite more scholars in support of this theory for many of the people most highly esteemed in this field have concluded that the Family Sagas are based to some extent on tradition among much else. I will quote only one of these people. Gabriel Turville-Petre discusses the background and the basis of Icelandic saga writing, and he continues thus:

> It need not be doubted that Icelanders of the eleventh and twelfth centuries used to tell stories for entertainment, and storytelling became a practised art among them. It is likely that some of the stories were concerned with Icelandic traditions.[3]

Following up these words, Turville-Petre illustrates further the oral traditions circulating in Iceland. In this connection, he particularly stresses that it might be instructive to compare the preservation of Icelandic tradition with that of Irish tradition more extensively than has been done hitherto. Later he says of Irish and Icelandic tales: "The Irish and Icelandic styles both appear to be literary rather than oral, and they have both been developed through long practice on parchment."[4]

These words refer to certain important stages in the development that presumably lies behind individual Icelandic sagas in their present form. We shall have to reckon with these entities when we attempt to get hold of any religious material dating back to the time of Old Norse paganism that may be lurking in the Icelandic sagas. Conditions will not have been favourable for the preservation of such matter in the cultural climate of a newly introduced faith resolutely and unequivocally opposed to anything not consistent with Christian belief. Consequently tradition that took shape in the days of Old Norse paganism, and actually bore its stamp, must have obtained a fixed form if they were to survive in the oral tradition after the Conversion. Their form could keep them alive, even if their content and message was at variance with the prevailing religion of the country. From this point on, the highest threshold of such traditions as these, was of course the force of creativity in which the

---

3   Turville-Petre 1975, 231.
4   Ibid, 233.

author of each Icelandic saga was at work. Authors could quite freely allow themselves to move the material around and arrange it to suit their own fancy. The transmitters of oral tradition were by contrast more or les bound to pass on the main facts of what they had heard.

Scraps of evidence of one sort or another bearing on Old Norse paganism can be perceived in very many sagas. This material varies greatly in value ranging from an obscure suggestion that a given hero worshipped one of the ancient gods rather than others, right up to complete narratives concerning sacred practices or even a fragment of an old and genuine myth. The authors of the Icelandic sagas were Christians, some of them probably with a clerical education and working in the service of the church. By the time they composed their works, Christianity had been dominant in all parts of the country for a good two hundred years. So doubtless, most or all of them were prejudiced against Old Norse paganism, as such, and indeed, it is questionable how far they understood it. Dag Strömbäck has drawn attention to the fact that memories of paganism were fast fading in thirteenth century Iceland, while at the same time, various features of popular superstition were thriving, untouched by the Conversion, or by the preaching of the church.[5]

I have for some time concentrated on investigating evidence of Old Norse paganism in the sagas. I have applied the method of research used in folkloristics and comparative religion. Where narratives of religious significance turn up in the sagas, I have tried to distinguish between two kinds: firstly, the sort that offers traces of pagan faith as it probably was when this religion flourished in Iceland in the tenth century, and secondly, the sort which reflects the folk beliefs or superstitions that actively persisted in Iceland during the eleventh, twelfth and thirteenth centuries. At times, the two are indistinguishable, but on other occasions it is possible to separate them.

In this lecture, I intend to deal with narratives which have religious implications in two Family Sagas: *Víga-Glúms Saga* and *Hrafnkels saga Freysgoða*. In both these sagas, we encounter material that bears the stamp of some sort of formulation in the tenth century.

---

5 Strömbäck 1935, 4.

Fragments of Old Norse mythology are apparent together with accounts of sacred rites and Old Norse religious observances. Some of this material shows signs of having been corrupted in the course of the eleventh – thirteenth centuries, and at times it has been contaminated by folk beliefs, which survived in full vigour after the Conversion. The first task is therefore to distinguish between motifs of pagan belief and folk belief as far as may be possible.

In both these sagas, a worship of the fertility god, Freyr, is an integral part of the story. In *Víga-Glúms saga*, the hero has to contend with worshippers of Freyr as has been shown in the previous chapter. In *Hrafnkels saga*, the hero is himself a worshipper of Freyr. Víga-Glúmr seems to have put his trust in Óðinn, the god of warfare and poetry. The same seems to be true of the enemies of Hrafnkell, the priest of Freyr, as far as we can deduce. But now, it is time to examine the religious motifs in each saga separately.

Many details to do with *Víga-Glúms saga* were given in the previous chapter and will not be repeated here. However, it might be noted that scholars have pointed out that the gifts of Vigfúss, Víga-Glúmr's grandfather, pertain to the worship of Óðinn. The spear was Óðinn's favourite weapon, and in myth and tradition, Óðinn is said to appear in a cloak, so the spear and the cloak actually express more about the beliefs of Víga-Glúmr than might at first appear. Descriptions of good luck gifts had a better chance of surviving the Conversion in oral tradition than accounts of outcried heathen worship of individual gods. In all ages, good luck gifts have been in happy accord with the concepts of folktales, whereas the various gods of Old Norse religion were taboo after the Conversion. For this reason, documentation of the gods could only survive in exceptional circumstances, or rather unusual records, while the good luck gifts retained their function and played their part in the development of the story.

As soon as Glúmr returned home to Iceland, he resumed the struggle against Þorkell the Tall and Sigmundr and pursued it under the banner of Óðinn, and the help of his good luck gifts. Further evidence of Glúmr's worship of Óðinn is that he cultivated poetry and many of his verses are incorporated in the saga. But, conversely, as the saga goes on, relations between Glúmr and Freyr became steadily worse. Glúmr and his mother had the right to cul-

tivate the cornfield at Vitazgjafi every other year, in turn with
Þorkell and Sigmundr. Now, the father and the son unjustly kept
the use of the field for two years in succession. As soon as Sig-
mundur set about reaping the field in the second autumn, Glúmr
accosted him and the events in the field are told like this:

> Síðan fór hann í feldinn ok tók spjótit í hǫnd sér. Síðan snarar hann
> at honum Sigmundi ok brá spjótinu, en hann spratt þegar upp í
> móti, en Glúmr hjó þegar í hǫfuð honum, ok þurfti Sigmundr eigi
> fleiri.[6]

> (Then he put on the cloak and took the spear in his hand. Next, he
> turned sharply on Sigmundr and brandished the spear. Sigmundr
> leapt up to meet him while Glúmr straight-faced struck at his
> head and this was quite enough for Sigmundr.)

Glúmr won the case arising from the killing and Þorkell had to
hand over his part of Þverá. The saga next tells of Þorkell the Tall
giving the ox as an offer to Freyr as was indicated in the previous
chapter.[7]

At this point, Þorkell the Tall disappears from the story, but
Freyr is said to have kept up the quarrel with Víga-Glúmr. The next
news of Freyr is in connection with the outlawry of Vigfúss, the son
of Víga-Glúmr:

> En hann mátti eigi heima vera fyrir helgi staðarins... ok helt
> Glúmr hann á laun. En því skyldu eigi sekir menn þar vera, at
> Freyr leyfði eigi, er hof þat átti, er þar var.[8]

> (Of him it is said that he could not live at home because of the
> concentrated nature of the place, and Glúmr kept him in hiding.
> Men under penalty were not admitted there because Freyr, deity to
> the temple there, did not allow it.)

This instance seems to hint at hostility between the gods Freyr
and Óðinn. Freyr appears here as a god of the legitimate order of

---

6 *ÍF* IX, 28.
7 *ÍF* IX, 34. Cf. p. 89.
8 *ÍF* IX, 66 Cf. pp. 89-90.

things, as is not unnatural for the god of fertility and peacefulness.[9] Óðinn is the opposite. I have already stated that Óðinn was the god of warfare and poetry, but his province often appears to have been wider. Georges Dumézil and others have pointed out that Óðinn was on the one hand the god of kings and ideal heroes, and on the other that of lawbreakers and men of violence, those who would stop at nothing and take by force what they could not get by lawful means.[10] In consequence, it follows logically that the rebellious elements of the community sought support from Óðinn, namely, those people who were asserting themselves by force, gaining possession of power or influence by all possible means. Víga-Glúmr seems to be an example of such a man.

In various parts of *Víga-Glúms saga*, there are passages which have been interpreted as undoubted instances of Glúmr's worship of Óðinn. There is the occasion when Vigfúss, son of Glúmr, had unlawfully stayed at Þverá or in the neighbourhood for three years, and a fight broke out near the farm. Glúmr and his men were getting the worst of it when a man in a leather cloak arrived and joined their side. Glúmr greeted him with the words: "Welcome, emblem of Óðinn". The saga indicates that this was his son, Vigfúss, in disguise. The term used is "Þundarbenda", which has been explained as sign or indication from Óðinn, and *Þundr* is one of the applications of Óðinn. Magnus Olsen thought that this story implied that Glúmr's son Vigfúss was a particular sign of good fortune, showing that Óðinn was on his side.[11]

There are other indications in *Víga-Glúms Saga* of a compact between Glúmr and Óðinn, of his close connection with this god and his hostility towards Freyr. After the battle just mentioned, Glúmr was made to swear an oath in three temples to the effect that he had not slain a named person in the fight. One of these temples was the temple of Freyr at Þverá. Glúmur arranged the phrasing of the oath in ambiguous terms so that it could be taken to mean

---

9 *ÍF* I, 313-315. Cf. Strömbäck 1975, 41; Jón Hnefill Aðalsteinsson 1978, 97 ff. and p. 69 above.

10 Dumézil 1973, 28ff. and references.

11 *ÍF* IX, 77. Olsen 1934, 92 ff.

either that he had not slain the man, or, that he had. The bystanders took the oath as meaning that Glúmr had not slain the man, and the ambiguity was not discovered until long after. Turville-Petre specifically connects this oathtaking with Óðinn, saying: "He followed Óðinn's example by swearing an ambiguous oath in three temples, one of which was the temple of Freyr."[12]

At this point in the story, Glúmr had given serious offence to Freyr three times over. He had committed triple sacrilege which was bound to demand retribution. He had killed a man in sacred field, he had housed a condemned man on holy ground and he had sworn an ambiguous oath in a sacred temple. It appears from the saga that Freyr had now had enough. When the case of homicide was brought a second time on grounds of the ambiguous oath, and people were setting off to the general assembly, the saga tells of the dream Glúmr had before he rode from home as is recaounted in the previous chapter.[13]

By now, Glúmr had parted with two of the good luck gifts from his maternal grandfather: the cloak and the spear. This time he lost the lawsuit and was forced to leave Þverá. He then made a final bid to avoid his departure from the farm. Einar, the new owner, had sent men to work. Glúmr suggested to him that he should put up a *váðmeiðr,* a pole for hanging out clothes, by the river. When they got home, they told Einar of this, and Einar then said:

> "Þat hygg ek, at við þann meið festi hann ykkr upp, en ætli at reisa mér níð."[14]

> ("In my opinion, he will string you up on his pole, and he plans to hoist an insult that is a *níð* to me.")

Níð was black magic, and it is several times mentioned in Old Norse sources, both before and after the Conversion. This kind of insult was for instance used against the missionaries who first preached Christianity in Iceland. One method of *níð* was to erect a *níðstöng*, a pole of infamy, and via this means, the insult was specif-

---

12 Turville-Petre 1964, 70.
13 ÍF IX, 87-88. Cf p. 90 above.
14 ÍF IX, 88-89.

ically directed against a given person. The message here alluded to is nevertheless unlike that generally understood in the description of *níð*. Scholars are therefore inclined to think that here we have a corruption in oral transmission, that is to say a method that was originally religious practice has now turned into sorcery. This sort of development is actually not unusual when an earlier religion has been abandoned. Such a conclusion also fits in very well with my earlier contention, that in the thirteenth century, people were far more familiar with various superstitions than the usage of Old Norse paganism. *Níð* was one of the practices which held good after the victory of Christianity. Therefore, it is in no way exceptional to find it a potent factor in a saga of the thirteenth century.[15]

Scholars have judged that the original nucleus of the tradition described here contained an account of a sacrifice to Óðinn. Glúmr's purpose in telling the workmen to set up a clothes pole was to hang them on it, and sacrifice them to Óðinn. Glúmr intended this sacrifice by hanging to test whether Óðinn might not prevent his forced ejection from Þverá. In support of this interpretation it has been pointed out that Óðinn was the "hanging god", the god of hanged men. Secondly, there are sources to show that Óðinn, more than any other god, was the recipient of human sacrifice. Thirdly, scholars have pointed to strong evidence that Glúmr was a devout Óðinn worshipper, as has been demonstrated here. Hence, it is a fair guess that the anecdote has the implications of an intended sacrifice to Óðinn.

But Víga-Glúmr did not succeed either in carrying out a supposed sacrifice to Óðinn, or in avoiding the fate of being himself thrown off Þverá. It is a point well worth observing, that Freyr comes out victorious in the struggle between divinities that can be glimpsed behind the events in *Víga-Glúms saga*. Strong reasons have been induced to show that a considerable fund of tradition about Víga-Glúmr was in circulation already in the tenth century and elements are still traceable in the saga. It would seem that people who were transmitting material of this sort, and cherishing it, were fully capable of grasping that the god of fertility, peace, and law and order, should come off victorious over the god of kings, warriors,

---

15 Almqvist 1967: "Nid" i *KLNM* XII, 295-299 and references.

rebels and poets. Tradition that set forth such truths also gave appropriate support to stability and lawfulness in the young legal system of tenth century Iceland.

Hrafnkels saga Freysgoða describes, among other things, the pagan practices of the hero, Hrafnkell the priest of Freyr, who lived at Aðalból in Hrafnkelsdalur:

> Hrafnkell elskaði eigi annat goð meir en Frey, ok honum gaf hann alla gripi sína hálfa við sik... Hrafnkell átti þann grip í eigu sinni, er honum þótti betri en annarr. Þat var hestr brúnmóáróttr at lit, er hann kallaði Freyfaxa sinn. Á þessum hesti hafði hann svá mikla elsku, at hann strengði þess heit, at hann skyldi þeim manni at bana verða, sem honum riði án hans vilja.[16]

> (Hrafnkell loved no god more than Freyr, and to Freyr had devoted a half share of all his greatest valuables. Hrafnkell possessed a treasure that he valued above all else. This was a brownish grey horse, with a dark stripe down the back. He called the horse his Freyfaxi. He gave half possession of this horse to his patron, Freyr. So devoted was he to this horse, that he swore an oath to be the death of anyone who rode it without his permission.)

In spite of strict warnings, Einar, Hrafnkell's herdsman, took the horse and rode it all day long. When he realeased the horse, says the saga:

> Hestrinn hleypr ofan aptir dalnum ok nemr eigi stað, fyrri en hann kemr á Aðalból. Þá sat Hrafnkell yfir borðum. Ok er hestrinn kemr fyrir dyrr, hneggjaði hann þá hátt. Hrafnkell mælti við eina konu, þá sem þjónaði fyrir borðinu, at hon skyldi fara til duranna, því at hross hneggjaði, − "ok þótti mér líkt vera gnegg Freyfaxa." Hon gengr fram í dyrrnar ok sér Freyfaxa mjök ókræsiligan. Hon sagði Hrafnkeli, at Freyfaxi var fyrir durum úti, mjök óþokkuligr. "Hvat mun garprinn vilja, er hann er heim kominn?" segir Hrafnkell. "Eigi mun þat góðu gegna." Síðan gekk hann út ok sér Freyfaxa ok mælti við hann: "Illa þykki mér, at þú ert þann veg til gǫrr, fóstri minn, en heima hafðir þú vit þitt, er þú sagðir mér til, ok skal þessa hefnt verða. Far þú til liðs þíns." En hann gekk þegar upp eptir dalnum til stóðs síns.[17]

---

16 *ÍF* XI 1950, 99-100.
17 Op. cit., 104.

(The horse galloped down up the valley, and never stopped until he reached Aðalból. Hrafnkell was sitting at a table, and when the horse came to the door, it neighed loudly. Hrafnkell told a woman waiting at the table to go to the door because a horse was neighing, - "and it seemed to me like the neigh of Freyfaxi". She went out to the door and saw Freyfaxi in a disgusting state. She told Hrafnkell that Freyfaxi was outside the door, utterly filthy. "What can the dear fellow mean by coming home", said Hrafnkell. "This spells no good". Then he went out and saw Freyfaxi and said to him: "I'm very sorry, my fosterling, that you have been treated so. But you had the sense to come home and tell me, and there will be a vengeance for this. Be off to your herd." So the horse went straight up the valley to his herd.)

The next day, Hrafnkell clothed himself in black, took his axe in his hand, and rode to the mountain pasture. When the herdsman confirmed that he had ridden Freyfaxi, Hrafnkell sank the axe in the herdsman's head and killed him. The herdsman's father obtained the support of Sámr, his brother's son, and the two of them brought a lawsuit against Hrafnkell for the killing. At the General Assembly they had the backing of two chieftains of the Westfjords quarter, Þorgeir and Þorkell, sons of Þjóstarr. With their help, Hrafnkell was condemned to full outlawry. The two sons of Þjóstarr then went with Sámr to Aðalból. They seized Hrafnkell and his men and treated them as follows:

Í túninu stóð útibúr. Af því ok heim á skálavegginn var skotit váðási einum... Þá taka þeir Hrafnkel ok hans menn ok bundu hendr þeira á bak aptr. Eptir þat brutu þeir upp útibúrit ok tóku reip ofan ór krókum, taka síðan knífa sína ok stinga raufar á hásinum þeira ok draga þar í reipin ok kasta þeim svá upp yfir ásinn ok binda þá svá átta saman.[18]

(In the home pasture stood an outhouse. From this building to the wall of the living quarters, they ran a pole for drying washing. Then they took Hrafnkell and his men and bound their hands behind their backs. Next, they broke open the shed and lifted a rope from a box. Then they took their knives and stabbed holes behind the men's hamstrings, threw them up across the pole and tied all eight together.)

18 Op. cit., 119-120.

This is how Hrafnkell and his men were left to hang until the confiscation court was convened. Then they were taken down. By then their eyes were shot with blood. Þorgeir invited Sámr to do as he pleased with Hrafnkell. Sámr granted life to Hrafnkell on condition that he went to live at a specific distance. Þorgeir was amazed that Sámr had spared Hrafnkell's life. He would be likely to regret it. The story then turns to Hrafnkell and describes how he settled in Fljótsdalur and set up a farm on a slender means, yet everything turned out to his advantage. This is how the saga puts it:

> Hrafnkell dró á vetr kálf ok kið in fyrstu misseri, ok hann helt vel, svá at nær lifði hvatvetna þat, er til ábyrgðar var. Mátti svá at kveða, at náliga væri tvau hǫfuð á hverju kvikindi. Á því sama sumri lagðisk veiðr mikil í Lagarfljót.[19]

> (Hrafnkell fed a calf and a kid throughout the winter in his first season. And his luck held, for almost every creature he risked came safe through. It could be said that each animal had pretty much two heads. That same summer, great shows of fish appeared in Lagarfljót.)

Once Hrafnkell's resurgence at Hrafnkelsstaðir has been described, the saga turns back to Hrafnkelsdalur, where the sons of Þjóstarr were still enjoying Sámr's hospitality. They wanted to take a look at the horses and they approved of all but Freyfaxi. Þorgeirr said it was only right that the one who owned him should receive him. So, the story continues:

> Þeir leiða nú hestinn ofan eptir vellinum. Einn hamarr stendr niðr við ána, en fyrir framan hylr djúpr. Þar leiða þeir nú hestinn fram á hamarinn. Þjóstarssynir drógu fat eitt á hǫfuð hestinum, taka síðan hávar stengr ok hrinda hestinum af fram, binda stein við hálsinn ok týndu honum svá.[20]

> (They led the horse down the meadows. There is a crag down beside the river, and in front of it a deep pool. The sons of Þjóstarr pulled a bag over the horse's head, then took long poles, and

---

19 Op. cit., 122.
20 Op. cit., 123-124. Cf. Jón Hnefill Aðalsteinsson: "Freyfaxahamarr", *Skáldskaparmál* 4 1997, 238-253.

pushed the horse over, having tied a stone around his neck, and so they destroyed it.)

Once Freyfaxi was disposed of, the building where Hrafnkell kept his idols was next in line.

> Þorkell vildi koma þar. Lét hann fletta goðin ǫll. Eptir þat lætr hann leggja eld í goðahúsit ok brenna allt saman.[21]

> (Þorkell wanted to go to the place. He had all the idols stripped of their valuables. Then he had the gods' temple set on fire, and the whole lot burnt up.)

Next we hear that the sons of Þjóstarr went off home. And this is how Hrafnkell reacted to their last exploit at Aðalból:

> Hrafnkell spurði austr í Fljótsdal, at Þjóstarssynir hǫfðu týnt Frey-faxa ok brennt hofit. Þá svarar Hrafnkell: "Ek hygg þat hégóma at trúa á goð," – ok sagðisk hann þaðan af aldri skyldu á goð trúa, ok þat efndi hann síðan, at hann blótaði aldri.[22]

> (Back in the east in Fljótsdalur, Hrafnkell heard that the sons of Þjóstarr had destroyed Freyfaxi and burnt the temple. He then replied: "I think it is a nonsense to believe in gods, and he declared that he would never believe in human gods and he was as good as his words, for he never again made a sacrifice.)

In the very next sentence we hear that Hrafnkell acquired wealth and respect, and built up a chieftainship over more men than he had had previously. It is said of Sámr that he retained the chief-tainship of Hrafnkell in Hrafnkelsdalur and the neighbourhood. Finally, we hear how Hrafnkell avenged himself on Sámr, and reclaimed his former dominance.

Hrafnkels saga describes events that would have taken place just before the middle of the tenth century. The saga is short and com-pact. Scholars once took this as an indication that it was composed early and was based on reliable tradition. These assumptions were overturned by Nordal in 1940 in his essay, "Hrafnkatla". There he

---

21 Op. cit., 124.
22 Op. cit., 124.

marshals reasons to show that the main events never took place and that two of the leading characters, the sons of Þjóstarr, never existed. According to him the saga was composed in about 1300 and was the work of an author who had no intention of telling a true story, but wanted rather to produce a work of fiction.[23]

In the last decades, Nordal's essay has decisively affected attitudes to *Hrafnkels saga*. His main theory, that the saga was the work of a man who was more of an artist than a historian, and treated his material freehand, has not been challenged, nor yet that the saga was written near 1300. On the other hand, some scholars have pointed out that the saga relies on tradition to a larger extent than Nordal assumed.

Knut Liestöl wrote in 1946 that in all probability the saga was based on ancient and reliable tradition for its religious content. In a book published in 1964, Turville-Petre wrote that he agreed with the main thesis of Nordal that *Hrafnkels saga* was a work of fiction, but, he says, the saga includes some motifs that are probably based on tradition.[24]

In the 1980s, some scholars have published works on this specific point, where they argue once again, that *Hrafnkels saga* is in some way based on tradition, some of it extending right back to the tenth century. The argument concerns the opening chapters where tradition differs from *Landnámabók*. But it also tackles the religious content of *Hrafnkels saga*.[25]

At present, the scholarly opinion on *Hrafnkels saga* is in broad outline that the saga is the work of an individual in the late thirteenth century, but it is based on narrative material assigned to the first half of the tenth century. Some of the material is evidently invention as far as persons in the saga goes, but some of it seems to be based on traditions which can be traced back to the tenth century. As things stand, it is time to scrutinise the religious events I have described, but first it is necessary to say a few words about the religion of tenth century Iceland according to the sources available.

The settlers who took land in Iceland in the late ninth and early

---

23 Sigurður Nordal 1940, 66ff.
24 Liestøl 1946, 94-110. Turville-Petre 1964, 167 and works there referred to.
25 Hofmann 1976, 19-36. Óskar Halldórsson 1976, 31ff. Jónas Kristjánsson 1978, 271-350.

tenth centuries were for the most part believers in Old Norse paganism. A very few Christian landtakers are mentioned in *Landnámabók*, but accompanied by the remark, that Christianity did not survive among their descendants. It is specifically stated that Iceland was completely heathen for a hundred years, which means almost hundred and twenty years. Once the land was fully settled around 930, its administration was regulated and a general assembly was founded and attended by chieftains from all parts of the country. Assemblies were set up in all quarters of the country. Three *goðar* or priests jointly conducted each assembly. *Goði* is etymologically related to the word "god", but it is a special technical term. The *goðar* had two functions. They kept control of the administration and at the same time, they took the lead in religious affairs. They controlled legal business at assemblies, and they presided over sacrifice in the temples and at assemblies. Each assembly was inaugurated by a sacrifice conducted by the goði who convened the assembly. He slaughtered the sacrificial animal at the assembly and moistened the holy ring in its blood. It was obligatory to take an oath on this ring for all men who had a case to bring, or had to bear witness or give judgement in lawsuits. Thus, there are reliable sources to show that the processes of government and the conduct of religious affairs were inextricably intertwined in tenth century Iceland, and absolute control of both lay in the hands of the *goðar*.[26]

It is essential to keep in mind these facts about religion when we come to assess the hereditary and often traditionally religious episodes of *Hrafnkels saga*. I will now examine these passages one after another and look at them in the light of religion. The first step is to discover whether such traditions could have existed in the tenth century, and whether they accord with the religious concepts of the period. If they do, it is not impossible that these passages describe accurate events although, of course, the fact cannot be proven in one way or other, but if these traditions are at variance with what we know of the religion of the tenth century, then we can discard them as inventions or as the incorrect records of a later age.

When the saga says that Hrafnkell had sworn to kill any man

---

26 Jón Hnefill Aðalsteinsson 1997a, 163-187 and works there referred to. Cf. pp. 35-57 above.

who rode Freyfaxi, scholars have taken it as an ancient motif, slightly corrupted. The horse was dedicated to Freyr, and therefore it was forbidden to ride him on pain of death. To support this hypothesis, people have referred to traditions about sacred horses which no men may ride. Such traditions are found, for instance, in Tacticus's *Germania* and in *The Saga of Saint Olaf* in *Flateyjarbók*.[27] This hypothesis seems to be correct, and the reasons given for supporting it are convincing.

In the *Germania* of Tacitus, it is specifically mentioned that religious authorities listened to the neighing and snorting of sacred horses and interpreted their findings as a message from the gods. There seems to be an example of the same practice when Freyfaxi galloped to the farm and complained about the sacrilege done to him. This story has no exact parallel in Old Norse literature, but it seems to accord perfectly with religious concepts now recognised in such cases. Thus there is no theoretical reason to deny that such an event could have taken place or that people believed it could have taken place. This story, in the form it assumes in *Hrafnkels saga* is the next best thing to a genuine myth of all the raw material in all the Icelandic sagas. The fertility god Freyr raises his voice in ringing tones and waits for an answer.

If these events are considered in a religious context, Hrafnkell had not only a clear moral right to kill the herdsman, he also had a legal right. And we should take note that his adversaries carried the case against him with violence at the General Assembly, not by normal, legal means.

Now let us consider the story of when Hrafnkell and his men were strung up on a clothes-pole. As before, there is no parallel in Old Norse literature. Anne Holtsmark suggested that this was a premeditated sacrifice to Óðinn and that Sámr and his companions carried their plan somewhat further than did Víga-Glúmr at Þverá.[28] Continuing with what I said about Óðinn as the god of heroes and warriors, it is not extravagant to imagine that Sámr was an Óðinn worshipper. His whole conduct involved a rebellion against the authority of the goði of the region.

In the light of what is known of sacrifice to Óðinn in the sphere

---

27 Tacitus: *Germania*, Ch. 11. *Flateyjarbók* I 1944, 445-449.
28 Holtsmark 1933, 111ff.

of Old Norse paganism, it is by no means extravagant to suppose that from Sámr's point of view, it was the obvious thing to sacrifice Hrafnkell to Óðinn. In this way, Sámr could conceivably ensure the favour of Óðinn and thus offset the sacrilege he had committed against the cult of Freyr, for after all, he had attacked the *goði* of Freyr who had done no more than observe the dictates of his faith, as he was bound to do, by avenging sacrilege at the command of Freyr. In the narrative itself, it looks as though Þorgeir, the *goði* of West-fjords, had also expected Sámr to carry out the process to its con-clusion, that he would kill the men, and so present them as a sacri-fice to Óðinn.

There is an allusion to this matter later on in the saga, when Sámr approaches the sons of Þjóstarr the second time, seeking for their support after Hrafnkell has got revenge on him. Þorgeir then refers to the previous business and declares he is not going to draw down Sámr's ill luck upon the two of them, himself and his brother. It was ill luck in the terms of Old Norse paganism to break faith with the gods and cheat them of sacrifice which had been proposed.

From what I have said, it is plain there is nothing in Old Norse paganism to prevent us from thinking that the stringing up of Hrafnkell and his men was intended as sacrifice. Various points of inner logic in the saga also support this interpretation. Of course, it is also possible to take the view that in terms of simple convenience, it would have been in Sámr's interest to destroy Hrafnkell and so get rid of a powerful adversary. Yet, it seems to me that the theological explanation strikes a deeper root into the subject matter of the saga.

The account of the destruction of Freyfaxi is far more difficult to fit into the conceptual world of Old Norse religion. Certainly, sacred horses were sacrificed in the time of Old Norse paganism, but at fes-tive ceremonies and accompanied by appropriate religion. This case is nothing of the sort. Turville-Petre commented on the incident, saying:

> This story is supported by Norwegian traditions, and might be regarded as a travesty of a sacrifice to Freyr. This was no ordinary horse, and the slaughterers acted as did many who executed witches and wizards who possessed the evil eye.[29]

---

29 Turville-Petre 1964, 254; 267. Cf. Jón Hnefill Aðalsteinsson 1997b, 249ff.

With these words, Turville-Petre got to the root of the matter as far as this saga is concerned, What he tells of here is alien to Old Norse religion. The story cannot be preserving a historical element in this particular form.

The description of how the gods were stripped of their clothes and how the temples were set on fire is likewise totally at variance with the religion of the period in which the story of Hrafnkell falls. Old Norse religion seems to have been dominant and unchallenged throughout pretty well all the tenth century in Iceland, and especially strong in the mid-century. The spiritual and temporal authorities, the *goðar*, sustained a faith, and it made no difference to the central issue whether they believed principally in Þórr, Freyr or Óðinn. It was a matter of varying accents. Moreover, it appears that idols of all three gods were to be found in most of the temples of which there is any record.[30] Never mind if individuals had their favourite gods, this group of gods always seems to have been regarded as one unit. It was a general rule to tolerate gods other than the one individually preferred, and yet here we are told of *goðar* who committed sacrifice in the temples, and burned another temple down, which at that time is simply impossible.

It is worth mentioning that just before the year 1000, a Christian missionary arrived in Iceland. He tried to demolish the temples and deface the idols. The General Assembly then passed a special law which imposed the heaviest penalties upon anyone who made unseemly attacks in word or action on the gods, on the idols, or sacred objects.[31]

The declarations of Hrafnkell are equally out to keeping with the history of religion in tenth century Iceland, that is to say, Hrafnkell's statement that he reckoned it folly to believe in gods and his following statement that he had ceased to sacrifice after he left Aðalból. The saga says that he went on being a *goði* and that the district under his authority was even wider than before. In his essay, "Hrafnkatla", Sigurður Nordal argues that the worship of Freyr might well have continued in Hrafnkell's family and that because of this, the account in the saga that Hrafnkell ceased holding sacrifices

---

30 Adam of Bremen lib. 4. XXVI (57ff.).
31 Jón Hnefill Aðalsteinsson 1978, 72 ff. and works referred to there.

and believing in the gods must be as fictional as that concerning the burning of the temple.[32] Of course, it must have been mandatory for a *goði* at this time to preside over sacrifices repeatedly throughout the year, and facing the ancient gods was likewise an essential precondition for taking part in the business of the assembly and sustaining authority. Here, the author may have been confused by the fact that the *goðar* retained their office and their secular power after the Conversion. The only change in their function when the Conversion took place was that the religious element in the office of *goði* became obsolete. Christian priests filled the gap.

I have here adduced certain examples from *Hrafnkels saga* which contradict the history of religion in tenth century Iceland. Accordingly, these incidents cannot be based on the tradition circulating in the country at this period. But I have still not touched on one passage in the sagas: the passage describing Hrafnkell's prosperity in the first year of his settlement at Hrafnkelsstaðir in Fljótsdalur. Telling of the fecundity of his livestock, the author graphically says that every animal kept over the winter survived, and there were just about "two heads on every creature". Additionally, there were fish for the taking in the lake of Lagarfljót as soon as Hrafnkell moved to Fljótsdalur.

It does not take a very sharp eye to see the hand of the god of fertility in the events described here. The aphoristic phrasing carries all the marks of having been coined already in the tenth century. It is natural to connect this description with Hrafnkell's worship of Freyr, as set forth in the beginning of the saga. He had never broken faith with Freyr. He had even gone so far as to kill a man with whom he was on good terms, and all for the sake of Freyr. His vow to the god had to take first place. The description of Hrafnkell's prosperity shows how the god rewarded his priest. Myth still held its ground, in spite of the fact that traditions about Hrafnkell had been on the go for three and a half centuries before they were dressed up in a fictional garb and thus recorded for life.

Translated by Joan Turville-Petre

---

32 Sigurður Nordal 1940, 32-33.

POSTSCRIPT

PROBABLY more has been written about *Hrafnkels saga* than about any other Icelandic family saga. The article that is republished here deals with only a few points. A booklet containing a bibliography of the editions of the saga (Icelandic and foreign) and most articles and books directly concerned with it was published in connection with a conference on *Hrafnkels saga* that was held in Egilstaðir in 1993.[33]

Of recent articles dealing with *Hrafnkels saga*, Guðrún Nordal's paper on "Trúskipti og písl í *Hrafnkels sögu*" from 1995 deserves special mention. In her article, Guðrún interprets the hanging of Hrafnkell from the washing pole as a firm of martyrdom. In this context, she writes:

> Að mínu viti hefðu áheyrendur sögunnar á þrettándu og fjórtándu öld skilið mætavel hvað hér var á seyði. Hinn heiðni Hrafnkell er settur í gervi píslarvottar, en það sem vantar á að aðgerðin verði fullkomnuð er að lífi hans er þyrmt og hann gengur frá vettvangi tvíefldur innra með sér.[34]

> (To the best of my knowledge, those listening to the story in the thirteenth and fourteenth centuries would have had a pretty good understanding of what was going on. The pagan Hrafnkell has been placed in the guise of a martyr, but what prevents the act from being perfect is that his life is spared and he leaves the area with his spiritual strength doubled.)

Guðrún goes on to examine Hrafnkell's success at Hrafnkelsstaðir, suggesting that the model for this description might be found in what is said in *Íslenska hómilíubókin* (The Icelandic Book of Homilies) about how Job's humility were rewarded by an increase in number of his domestic animals and servants.[35]

To my mind, however, these considerations by no means rule out the fact that the accounts in question might have roots in an oral legand from the tenth century, in which the hanging was interpreted as being a sacrifice made to Óðinn, in which the god was cheated of his victim, and where

---

33 *Bókfræði Hrafnkels sögu* 1993. See also Jón Hnefill Aðalsteinsson 1997b, 238-239.
34 Guðrún Nordal 1995, 102.
35 Op. cit., 103.

Hrafnkell's success was understood in terms of a blessing granted by Freyr to his servant in answer to the steadfast loyalty he had shown his god.[36]

Stories and legends are always bound to be interpreted in the light of the ruling ideology at any one time. This naturally applies to the subject matter of many Icelandic sagas, and not least to the more recent sagas like *Hrafnkels saga*. I have elsewhere given some explanation of the possible changes that such a legends might have gone through between the tenth and thirteenth centuries.[37]

Ágrip

Goðsögur og helgisiðir í Glúmu og Hrafnkötlu

L EIFAR GOÐSAGNA og helgisiðafrásagna í tveimur Íslendingasögum, *Víga-Glúms sögu* og *Hrafnkels sögu Freysgoða* er viðfangsefni ritgerðarinnar. Í inngangi er í stuttu máli vikið að stöðu rannsókna á Íslendingasögum almennt og vitnað til marktækra fræðimanna á þeim vettvangi. Síðan er sérstaklega hugað að því hvort arfsagnaefni sem sögurnar kunna að byggja á verði hugsanlega rakið aftur til tíundu aldar. Í framhaldi er kannað hvort menjar goðsagna eða frásagna af helgisiðum kunni að leynast í umræddu sagnaefni.

Í *Víga-Glúms sögu* er að finna talsvert fornt efni úr norrænum goðsögum og frásögur sem rekja má til fornra helgisiða. Söguhetjan, Víga-Glúmur, virðist hafa alist upp í trú á Frey og helgi Freys og áhrifa hefur samkvæmt sögunni gætt í ríkum mæli á ættarsetrinu, Þverá. Þegar Víga-Glúmur hafði snúist til Óðinsdýrkunar eftir dvöl hjá víkingnum afa sínum í Noregi átti hann í útistöðum við sambýlismenn sína sem dýrkuðu Frey staðfastlega og færðu honum fórnargjafir. Þeirri baráttu lauk með því að Víga-Glúmur neyddist til að hverfa frá Þverá.

Þau trúaratriði sem hér hafa verið rakin eru skýr í sögunni og virðast

---

36 Jón Hnefill Aðalsteinsson 1971, 45-46.
37 Jón Hnefill Aðalsteinsson 1997a, 81-103.

---

*This article is a slightly altered version of a paper read at the Hebrew University in Jerusalem on April 5 1987. It was originally published in *Tímarit Háskóla Íslands* 1987, under the title: "Norrænar goðsögur í *Glúmu* og *Hrafnkötlu*" (Old Norse Myths in *Glúma* and *Hrafnkatla*).

ekki að ráði afbökuð frá upphaflegri gerð. Höfundur sögunnar heldur þeim
þó ekki fram til að skýra atburðarás eða gang mála. Þau eru því nánast
óvirkar sagnleifar í bakgrunni sögunnar.

Í *Hrafnkels sögu Freysgoða* er miklum mun dýpra á trúarsögulega efninu
en í *Víga-Glúms sögu*. Hrafnkell er í upphafi sögunnar sagður einlægur
Freysdýrkandi og ætti hann samkvæmt því að hafa verið friðsemdarmaður.
En það var öðru nær samkvæmt sögunni, því að honum er lýst sem
harðskeyttum og ófyrirleitnum vígamanni. Upprunaleg helgisiðafrásögn
virðist þó leynast í lýsingunni á því er Freyfaxi rann til bæjar og hneggjaði
og Hrafnkell talaði til hans og drap síðan smalamanninn sem hafði van-
helgað hestinn. Aðrar frásagnir sögunnar sem víkja að guðum og átrúnaði
eru óljósari, en forn goðsögn um blessun frjósemisguðsins gæti þó leynst
að baki þar sem greint er frá því að tvö höfuð hafi verið á hverju kvikindi
á Hrafnkelsstöðum og mokveiði í Lagarfljóti.

Í *Hrafnkels sögu Freysgoða* er áberandi í hve mikilli andstöðu sumar
trúarsagnir sögunnar eru við þau viðhorf í trúarefnum sem ætla má að hafi
verið ríkjandi á sögutímanum. Goðar eru sagðir hafa átt hlut að því að
brenna hof, brjóta goðamyndir og farga helgum hesti sem meinvætt, en
síðan haldið trúarlegum embættisskyldum eins og ekkert hafi í skorist.
Þetta ósamræmi veldur því að óhugsandi má telja að samfelldar sagnir séu
undirstaða sögunnar. Er marktækur munur á *Hrafnkels sögu Freysgoða* og
Víga-Glúms sögu hvað þetta áhrærir.

Giants and Elves in Mythology and Folktales

I

THE PRINCIPAL sources of Old Norse Mythology are Eddic poetry, scaldic verse, the *Prose Edda* of Snorri Sturluson and *Heimskringla*, as well as other works which are less important here. The Eddic poems differ in age, but at least some of them date from the period before the Conversion. Many scaldic verses are likewise of this period. Snorri's *Prose Edda* and *Heimskringla* on the other hand were written early in the thirteenth century. So in their record of mythology we may on the whole expect to find greater corruption and alteration of the Old Norse religion which has been handed down in form of folk narrative than we can expect to find in the poems of the Edda.

At the beginning of my paper I shall set out to compare material in the Eddic poems and in Snorri's *Prose Edda*. For this purpose I have chosen two strophes of *Vǫluspá* which appear in both these works. In the Eddic poem *Vǫluspá* there is a description of how Gullveig was thrice burnt and three times reborn (st. 21); next how the seeress Heiðr raised her voice in sorcery and incantation (st. 22). The two strophes following tell how the gods went to sit on their judgement-seats, and consulted each other about tribute and compensation (st. 23). It is described how Óðinn declared war by hurling his spear over the troop of enemies, how the wall of the gods' citadel was breached and how the Vanir (the hostile gods) held the field by sorcery (st. 24). Next it says (in sts 25 and 26):

Þá gengo regin ǫll	Then all the powers
á rǫcstóla	went to their judgement seats,
ginnheilog goð,	the most holy gods,
ok um þat gættuz,	and took counsel about this:
hverir hefði lopt alt	who they were who had filled
lævi blandit	the sky with guile,
eða ætt iǫtuns	and had given over the
Óðs mey gefna.	bride of Óðr to the race of giants.

Þórr einn þar vá	Þórr alone struck out,
þrunginn móði,	swollen with rage –
hann sjaldan sitr,	seldom does he stay quiet
er hann slíct um fregn;	when he hears of such doings.
á genguz eiðar,	Oaths were broken,
orð oc særi,	declarations and convenants,
mál oll meginlig,	all the mighty contracts
er á meðal fóro.[1]	sealed between them.

These two strophes of *Voluspá* are incorporated in Snorri's *Prose Edda*; Snorri sets them in the context of a long story. The story recounts the origin of Óðinn's horse Sleipnir. A craftsman came to the gods and offered to make them a powerfully built stronghold and to complete the work over one winter; in return, he was to be rewarded with Freyja, the sun and the moon. He was to have no man's help in his work; but on Loki's advice he was allowed the use of his horse Svaðilfari for moving materials. The horse pulled along incredibly large boulders, and as summer approached it became clear that the work could be completed in the agreed time. The gods now realised their hopeless position and brought pressure to bear on Loki, until he promised to delay the work. Next evening a mare came out of the woods and whinnied to the horse. The horse at once ran after her, so the smith lost his help and was unable to finish the building in the set time. The builder flew into a giant-rage, and when the gods saw he was a mountain-giant they did not honour their oaths. They called upon Þórr, who killed the builder with his hammer Mjǫllnir. Loki's business with Svaðilfari had been of such kind that in due course he bore a foal, and that was Sleipnir.[2]

Snorri places the strophes I have quoted at the end of the aforementioned chapter. They were to cast more light on the state of affairs as the gods sat in council thinking out some way of preventing the builder from completing his work. The wide discrepancy between Snorri and the beginning of these strophes in *Voluspá*[3] has often led scholars to suggest that Snorri either misunderstood the poem, or otherwise distorted the sources at his disposal – inten-

---

1   *Edda. Die Lieder des Codex Regius* 1983, 6.
2   Snorri Sturluson 1931: *Edda*, 45 ff.
3   Turville-Petre 1964, 136-7.

tionally or not. On the other hand, Gabriel Turville-Petre has observed that maybe Snorri was not guilty of either misunderstanding or distortion since the account that Snorri offers does not actually contradict *Vǫluspá*. There remains the separate point that Snorri may not have taken all the material of this story from the poem; there is a strong possibility that here he is trying to adjust divergent sources, as he does every now and again. Then Snorri's narrative would contain a common folktale motif and other material that was never likely to have been in *Vǫluspá*.

There is a widespread story about a man who makes a compact with a builder to set up a church or other large building within a given time. The reward claimed by the builder is sometimes the man's soul, his son, his eyes or other precious things, sometimes the sun and moon. The man who strikes this bargain commonly takes to stratagems or trickery to avoid paying the agreed price. In this class falls the story of Bishop Laurentius, who entered into this kind of agreement to have the cathedral church in Lund in Sweden built. He pledged his eyes or the sun and moon as a payment.[4] In an Icelandic folktale about the building of the church at Reynir, the landowner promised his son to the builder.[5]

What Snorri has to say over and above *Vǫluspá* goes beyond folktale material. He gives additionally an account of Loki changing himself into a mare and luring away the horse Svaðilfari, with the result that the gods were able to escape paying the agreed price. The *Shorter Vǫluspá* states that Sleipnir was begotten on Loki by Svaðilfari,[6] but it is improbable that Snorri based his whole story on this one fact. What we have here is a myth of shape- and sex-change which has been combined with folktale motifs.

The folktale motifs in Snorri's story deserve particular attention. They show how early the mythology of Old Norse religion was infiltrated by various folklore motifs. This was no more than might be expected once the myths were no longer regarded as holy and true, while continuing to be an element of cultural entertainment. But the blending of myths with folktale motifs means that we must

---

4   Holbek and Piø 1979, 278-280.
5   Jón Árnason I 1961, 57-58.
6   *Sæmundar-Edda. Eddukvæði* 1926, 215.

move with caution when investigating this material. Special care must be taken not to associate too readily the original mythology of Eddic poems with the mythological material in Snorri's *Prose Edda*, which has been infiltrated with folklore motifs. We should in all seriousness be wary of following various scholars who have accepted folklore in Snorri's *Prose Edda* as a simple addition to the material of *Vǫluspá*.[7]

II

Giants are often mentioned in Eddic poetry. In *Vǫluspá* the seeress starts off by saying that she can remember the giants. According to the same poem, the first time they visited the gods was when three vigorous (*ámáttkar*) giantesses came to Ásgarðr.[8] Certain Eddic poems discourse at large upon the intelligence and knowledge of the giants. In *Hávamál* (The Words of the High One) Óðinn says that he visited the ancient giant, and it seems that he acquired great wisdom on that occasion. Later in the same poem Óðinn declares that he learnt nine mighty spells from his renowned maternal uncle, who was a giant.[9] But nowhere is the deep-seated wisdom and great learning of the giants more clearly expressed than in *Vafþrúðnismál* (The Words of Vafþrúðnir). Óðinn sought out the all-wise giant Vafþrúðnir to learn ancient wisdom from him. Once the giant had tested Óðinn and ascertained that he was worth an exchange of words, he recited to him the mythology of the origin of all things, the secrets of the giants and of the gods, the creation of the world and the gods, and the eventual end.[10]

Enmity between the gods and giants is also described in some Eddic poems, and in Snorri's *Prose Edda* there are many tales which display the hostile relationship in more detail. It is Þórr in particular who comes to blows with the giants and defends Ásgarðr, the dwelling of the gods, against them. This feud is mentioned among other matters in *Hymiskviða* (The Lay of Hymir) and *Þrymskviða* (The Lay of Þrymr).[11]

---

7   *Eddukvæði* 1968, 80.
8   *Edda. Die Lieder des Codex Regius* 1983, 1.
9   Ibid, 33; 40. See further pp. 21-22 above.
10 Ibid, 45 ff.
11 Ibid, 88 ff; 111 ff.

In spite of this, at some time a different, normally much more friendly relationship cleary also existed between the gods and giants. For example, the daughters of giants were thought to be the loveliest of women; many myths describe the gods seeking them in marriage or at any rate soliciting their favours. Þórr begot a son on a giant's daughter, Óðinn slept with Gunnlöð, Freyr married Gerðr, daughter of the giant Gymir, and Skaði was given first to Njǫrðr and afterwards to Óðinn. Giants in turn often lusted after Freyja and wanted to take her in marriage as is described among other things in *Þrymskviða.*[12] Dissent and struggle between gods and giants can sometimes be attributed to these love-affairs.

The giants of the Eddic poems and Snorri's *Prose Edda* have successors under various names in folktales of later ages. Sometimes a giant is called *jǫtunn*, as before, sometimes *risi*. Then there are trolls and ogresses (*trǫll. þurs, gýgr* or *flagð*). The individual features and characteristics of these beings have also changed to some extent. It certainly comes out in folktales of recent times that giants are reckoned to be clever. The giant of Torsjö (the Lake of Þórr), according to a Swedish folktale, was so clever and wise as to solve the most complicated questions. A merchant was so impressed by the giant's wisdom that he went to him to acquire knowledge.[13] Here we have the same motif as when Óðinn learnt from the giants in Old Norse myths.

An Icelandic folktale tells of a giant living in Bládalur who was exceptionally wise and clever. He understood everything both far and near, and could find an answer to all questions that were beyond the capacity of others. This giant also knew the purpose of men before a word was spoken.[14]

The stories just mentioned are among the exceptions in the class of giant- and troll-stories of recent times. In some stories trolls are said to be very stupid, and giants and trolls are usually represented in the shape of the huge and terrible adversaries of Þórr found in Eddic poems and Snorri's *Prose Edda*. One of the oldest folktales of trolls on record alludes to dealings between Þórr and the giants. It

---

12 Ibid, 33: 77; 111 ff. Snorri Sturluson 1931: *Edda*, 30 ff; 103. See further pp. 22-24 above.
13 *Svenska folksagor* 1981, 243 ff.
14 Jón Árnason IV 1956, 497 ff.

occurs in a twelfth century work about King Ólafr Tryggvason of Norway. This story describes how King Ólafr sailed along the Norwegian coast, and took on board Ása-Þórr himself. He gave the king news of this and that, and incidentally spoke of his own doings:

> "Herra land þetta er ver siglum firir var bygt forðum af risum nocquorum. En þat barsc at at þeir risarnir fengu nocquorn braðan bana oc dó þeir sua at eigi varð fleira eptir en konur ij... oc laust ec þer til bana."[15]

> ("Sire," he says, "the land we are sailing past was once inhabited by some giants. But it happened the giants were stricken with a sudden plague, and died out, until the only survivors were two women... and I battered them to death.")

The heroic valour of Þórr is here shown in an humorous light. All it involved was doing away with two helpless women who had lost all their kinsmen. But in this story Þórr seems to be boasting of having carried out a mighty achievement.

The harm done by trolls is often the subject of folktales. At times they are said to have mounted horses behind the riders, so as to get across brooks or rivers. They made themselves invisible, but the horses became "troll-ridden" as the saying goes: they suffered a kind of paralysis or general weakness. Then folktales tell how trolls have attacked people up in the mountains, trying to steal food or valuables from them, sometimes seizing men themselves for their pot, for trolls were thought to be man-eaters. The defence against trolls was to get to church and ring the bells; after all, they were heathens and firmly against the Christian faith.[16]

Some Icelandic folktales of trolls tell of their falling in love with humans. Ogresses are mostly concerned here, rather than giants. The trouble was that people lured away by ogresses are generally too small to mate with them. So they are smeared in grease and pulled out to make them longer. These men save themselves by asking for some rare and distant delicacy, such as shark flesh twelve years old. While the ogress is getting hold of this, they succeed in escaping.[17]

---

15 Oddur Snorrason 1932, 173-4.
16 Jón Árnason I 1961, 136 ff.
17 Ibid, 182 ff.

A frequent motif in Icelandic troll-stories is the good faith of trolls, and their kindness to those who treat them well. "Trolls' good faith" (*tröllatryggð*) is the tag applied to people notable for reliability and consideration. This motif points to statements in the Eddic poems and Snorri's *Prose Edda*, which say that the word of giants can be trusted no matter what happens. The gods broke their oaths, according to *Vǫluspá* and Snorri's *Prose Edda*, while the giants kept their word and paid for their good faith with their lives. The good faith of trolls comes out especially well in an Icelandic folktale, in the words of the trollwife Hallgerður of Bláfell. A man from the northern part of the country was sent across the mountains to the bishopric of Skálholt, because the people of the district had lost count of time and could not fix Christmas Day. On the way the man came across the troll who commented:

> "Hefði hann Kristur Máríuson unnið eins mikið fyrir okkur tröllin eins og þið segið að hann hafi unnið fyrir ykkur mennina þá hefðum við ekki gleymt fæðingardeginum hans."[18]

> ("If Christ son of Mary had done so much for us trolls as you say he did for you men, we certainly shouldn't have forgotten his birthday.")

It seems here that the age-old characterisation of giants and their nature has been preserved in folktales right down to the last century.

A typical feature of tales about trolls in Icelandic folktale collections is that the motifs of mythical trolls and giants have appreciably faded. Accounts of gods and giants in the mythical Eddic poems are full of life, whether their dealings are friendly or hostile. Things are quite different in the troll stories of later ages. Here the stories are always located at a great distance from the narrator, and are formed of loose-knit traditional patterns. Historical legends of trolls are rare, and in any case trolls never seem to have been a living reality in Icelandic folk belief or folk culture. The principal stories involving trolls are place-name anecdotes or explanations of place-names; they occur when some feature of the landscape suggests trolls or other huge beings. Of the same kind are explanatory tales

---

18 Ibid, 151.

connected with large boulders or cliffs standing in isolation. Stories then tell us that these rocks have been hurled a great distance by trolls.[19]

III

Elves are often mentioned in the mythical Eddic poems. *"Hvat er með ásom?/ hvat er með álfom?"* ("How is it with the Æsir? How is it with elves?") asks the seeress in *Vǫluspá* (st. 48); and time and again the Æsir (gods) and the elves are named together in these poems. It appears that elves were especially associated with fertility cults, and indeed in *Grímnismál* (The Words of Grímnir) it is said that Freyr, the god of fertility, was given the realm of elves when he cut his first tooth.[20] Several early written sources mention sacrifice to elves, stating in so many words that elves received sacrifices. It is sometimes said that these sacrifices took place at the time of the Winter Nights, which goes still further to support the idea that they were associated with the cult of fertility.[21]

Old Icelandic texts mention elves in Iceland. In these works we also hear of beings which appear to be closely related to elves. Of this kind are the land spirits (who appear in many contexts) and the ármaðr, or fertility spirit who is said to have protected the cattle and the household of farmers.[22]

Icelandic folktale collections have numerous stories of elves, and their dealings with men are eventful. The document called "huldu-manna genesis" tells of the origin of elves. The terms *huldufólk* (hidden people) and *álfar* (elves) are used interchangeably for these creatures as time goes on. The elves show good will towards men and seek their support; but if they are offended they avenge themselves. The elves had a habit of luring young children away, or exchanging old shrunken elf-men for babies. Also they used tricks to gain human companionship: hidden people called *ljúflingar* (favourites)

---

19 Jón Hnefill Aðalsteinsson 1989, 187. See further Einar G. Pétursson 1997, 61 ff. where a different view is expressed.

20 *Edda. Die Lieder des Codex Regius* 1983, 187.

21 *ÍF* XXVI 1941, 20. *ÍF* VI 1943, 50.

22 Jón Hnefill Aðalsteinsson 1985b, 115-120.

sought the love of women, and elf women fell in love with humans.[23]

A common motif in accounts of the association between human men and elf women is seen in the story of two men, one older and the other younger, who go to visit two elf women; these offer them good food and make up beds for them beside themselves. The elder man, who is often a priest, does well in his love-making; but the younger man somehow goes astray in his courtship of the younger woman. For this reason he is unlucky for the rest of his life, and the ill-luck runs in his family for a long time.[24]

In these stories it is the unquestioned authority of elf women that comes out strongly. They not only manage the house where the two men are made welcome but also take the lead in all dealings that occur. Once these men have resorted to the elf women, their good fortune and the whole of their futures are in the women's power. They appear as deities and arbiters of fate.

Much the same can be said of the other dealings between elves and humans that appear in traditions and folktales down to recent times. For example, one can tell of a young man who dreamt that a woman came and asked him to accompany her. In his dream he went along with her, but then lost heart and turned back. Some nights later he dreamt of the same woman, who said to him,

> "Illa gjörðir þú Jón er þú ekki vildir fara með mér seinast. Skaltu vita að ég leitaði þín af heilum hug og í nauðsyn minni. Dóttir mín lá á gólfi og mátti ekki fæða nema mennskur maður færi um hana höndum, og hefðirðu orðið hinn mesti gæfumaður ef þú hefðir leyst mig og hana af þessu vandkvæði sem nú hefur dregið hana til dauða með miklum harmkvælum. Væntir mig að þér snúist hér eftir flestir hlutir til mótgangs og armæðu og værirðu þó verra af mér maklegur."[25]

("You did wrong, Jón, when you would not come with me recently. You should know that I came for you in pure good faith in my hour of need. My daughter was in labour and could not be

---

23 Jón Árnason I 1961, 6 ff.
24 Ibid, 79-80. Cf. Guðrún Bjartmarsdóttir 1982, 319-336.
25 Ibid, 21-22.

brought to give birth unless a human ran his hands over her. You would have been the most fortunate of men if you had delivered both of us from the peril that has now caused her death in great suffering. I foresee that henceforth most things will go against you and bring you sorrow, and yet you deserve even worse at my hands.")

This story plainly shows that the person approached has no way out of the situation. The elves are hard to deal with. They reward generously, but also they get their own back cruelly. And wherever they strike, people have something to show for it.

Yet at the same time sometimes folktales and traditions make mention of exceptional goodwill being shown to human beings by the elves, who do favours without any sign that such favours have been deserved. One woman was alone at night at farm in Iceland when she felt the onset of labour pains and lighted a lamp. Soon after, an unknown woman arrived and offered to help her. The woman accepted, and the other attended to her, washed and swaddled the baby and laid it in bed beside the mother. This woman was never seen again. It was supposed she was an elf woman who lived in the elf-hillock that stood near the farm.[26]

The belief in elves is still fully alive in Iceland. Some years ago, a student in the Folklore Studies Department of the University of Iceland told me of an occasion when she was small, playing with her brothers and sisters beside the farm where she was born and brought up. They saw a woman dressed in blue on the far side of a little brook that ran there. At first they thought that this was their mother, but when they ran towards the woman, she disappeared. The children then ran indoors, and found their mother at work; she had not been out of doors.

I could quote many similar incidents in Iceland, where people declare that elves were concerned. It is especially common to attribute various kinds of soil-disturbance to elves, in particular when landslides are brought on by building work or roadmaking. There are recent instances in Iceland of roads being diverted to avoid

---

26 Ibid, 26-27.

138

an elf-hillock; there are also examples of road-works being delayed for a time, while the elves are given a chance to move house.[27]

In Reykjavík, there are several boulders reputed to be the home of elves. Fifty years ago one of these boulders was to be blown up so that a new henhouse could be built on the site. As soon as this decision was taken, the hens gave up laying and before long they were not yielding one single egg. Tests showed that the hens were healthy and nothing was wrong with their feed, so it was decided to abandon the idea of blowing up the boulder. The day after this decision was taken, the hens began to lay once again, and before long the egg-yield regained its former level.[28]

Another boulder in Reykjavík was moved with the ready agreement of the elven occupants out of the line of a proposed road into a garden where it can still be seen. The City Engineer gave the details of this removal in a recent television interview.[29]

The examples given above show that the elves, the associates of the Æsir in the days of the Old Norse religion, are still alive and kicking in the realm of Icelandic belief. In all probability they can look forward to a long life to come.

Translated by Joan Turville-Petre

---

27 Sigurður Nordal 1972, xx ff. Cf. Valdimar Tr. Hafstein 1995, 24-39; 45-49.
28 Árni Óla 1968, 29ff.
29 An interview in the Icelandic television 1989.

---

*This paper was read at the 9th Congress of the International Society for Folk-Narrative Research, Budapest, on 10-17 June, 1989. It was originally published in *Arv, Scandinavian Yearbook of Folklore*, Vol. 46, under the title "Folk Narrative and Norse Mythology".

Ágrip

Jötnar og álfar í goðsögum og þjóðsögum

FORNT GOÐSAGNAEFNI sem að einhverju leyti hefur varðveist í þjóð-sögum síðari tíma er viðfangsefni þessarar ritgerðar. Fyrst er borið saman efni úr goðakvæði frá tíundu öld og hliðstæð frásögn í *Eddu* Snorra Sturlusonar frá fyrri hluta 13. aldar. Eru leiddar líkur að því að þar sem á milli ber hafi bæði þjóðsagnaminni og óskylt goðsagnaefni blandast frásögn Snorra. Vakin er sérstök athygli á nauðsyn þess að greina slíkt viðbótarefni til hlítar áður en því er aukið við goðakvæðin til fyllingar því sem þar þykir ábótavant.

Þá er vikið sérstaklega að jötnum og álfum, þeim verum sem sam-kvæmt norrænu goðakvæðunum höfðu mest samskipti við goðin til forna og gengu þeim næst. Er hugað að hlut jötna og álfa í þjóðsögum síð-ari alda og einkenni þeirra þar borin saman við lýsingar sem gefnar eru á þeim í fornkvæðunum.

Jötnar goðakvæðanna fornu birtast stundum undir jötunsheitinu í þjóðsögum síðari tima en oftar bera þeir heitin *risi, tröll, þurs, gýgur* eða *flagð*. Í örfáum þjóðsögum eru risar sagðir margfróðir eða hundvísir, en oftast eru þeir þó taldir mjög heimskir í þjóðsögunum. Tröll þjóðsagnanna eru á hinn bóginn rómuð fyrir orðheldni og þau eru raungóð þeim sem vel víkja að þeim. Mynd trölla er að öðru leyti fremur óskýr í íslenskum þjóð-sögum og þau hafa lifað lengst sem stórgerðar mannsmyndir í kennileitum örnefna.

Álfar virðast hafa verið mjög nátengdir goðunum til forna, einkum frjósemisgoðum. Á Íslandi er álfa getið í fornum heimildum en er stundir líða fram eru heitin álfar og huldufólk notuð jafnhliða og sammerkt um þennan hóp yfirnáttúrulegra vera. Samkvæmt þjóðsögum síðari alda var huldufólk mönnum að öðru jöfnu vinveitt. Huldufólkið leitaði stundum á náðir manna, einkum álfkonur í barnsnauð og það launaði ríkulega ef vel var við brugðist, en hefndi sín grimmilega ef bón var neitað.

Margar þjóðsögur segja frá ástum manna og huldufólks. Algengustu minnin eru annars vegar sögur af ástum kvenna og ljúflinga og hins vegar sögur af heimsókn eldri karlmanns og yngri til tveggja álfkvenna sem þeir eiga ástarsamband við ef allt fer að sköpuðu.

Trúin á álfa og huldufólk lifir góðu lífi á Íslandi enn þann dag í dag. Kemur það einkar berlega í ljós þegar um framkvæmdir við mannvirkjagerð eða þjóðvegalagningu er að ræða þar sem hrófla þarf við meintri álfabyggð. Árið 1989 greindi borgarverkfræðingurinn í Reykjavík frá því í sjónvarpsviðtali, að steini sem ryðja þurfti úr vegi í borginni hefði verið lyft gætilega inn í næsta húsagarð með góðu samþykki íbúa steinsins, álfanna.

Wrestling with a Ghost
in Icelandic Popular Belief

I

A WRESTLING MATCH with a ghost or struggle with a revenant is an ancient motif in Old Norse literature. It appears, for instance, in the *Historica Danorum* of Saxo, in the Sagas of Icelanders, and in the Heroic Sagas (*fornaldarsögur*). This motif also occurs in Icelandic folk-tales recorded in the nineteenth and twentieth centuries.

Here I shall turn first to the oldest accounts of wrestling with a ghost, and attempt to establish their age and the features they have in common. Afterwards some of the latest evidence for this occurrence will be considered. As far as the latest tales go, an attempt will be made to estimate to what extent the narrators and recorders believed in the incident.

An ancient account of wrestling with a ghost is the story of how Hrómundr Gripsson entered the mound of Þráinn and wrestled with the mound-dweller. This tale is first mentioned in the description given in *Þorgils saga ok Hafliða* of the wedding-feast at Reykjahólar in the year 1119. *Þorgils saga ok Hafliða* is dated to the first decades of the thirteenth century,[1] and the description of the wedding entertainment has the following details:

> Hrólfr frá Skálmarnesi sagði sǫgu af Hrǫngviði víkingi ok frá Ólafi liðsmannakonungi ok haugbroti Þráins ok Hrómundi Gripssyni ok margar vísur með. En þessarri sǫgu var skemt Sverri konungi, ok kallaði hann slíkar lygisǫgur skemtiligstar, ok þó kunna menn at telja ættir sínar til Hrómundar Gripssonar. Þessa sǫgu hafði Hrólfr sjálfr saman setta.[2]

---

1   Jakob Benediktsson in *KLNM* XX 1976, 384-85 and works referred to there. See further Foote 1984, 65-83 and works referred to there.

2   *Sturlunga saga* 1906-11, 22.

(Hrólfr of Skálmarnes told a story about the viking Hrǫngviðr, Ólafr "king of hosts" and the mound-breaking of Þráinn and Hrómundr Gripsson, accompanied by many verses. This story was used to entertain King Sverrir, and he maintained that such fables [lying tales] were the most amusing; but all the same there are people who can trace their descent from Hrómundr Gripsson. Hrólfr composed this story himself.)

This account has occupied many scholars. One question among others that arise is how far the description of the wedding at Reykjahólar is based on reliable traditions where the substance of the entertainment is concerned. Ursula Brown and Peter Foote are inclined to think it reliable.[3] Klaus von See opposed, but Peter Foote has answered his objections.[4] Here there is not space to pursue this discussion, but on balance it seems that the author of *Þorgils saga ok Hafliða* had access to traditions about the wedding-feast at Reykjahólar and what went on there. The discussion has lately been taken up by Judith Jesch, and I refer readers to what she has to say.[5]

In *Þorgils saga ok Hafliða,* it emerges that Hrómundr Gripsson was a historic character. There are sources that name him as son of Gunnlǫð, daughter of Hrókr the Black and Gripr (Greipr); among those who could trace their ancestry to Hrómundr was the settler Ingólfr of Reykjavík, who according to *Landnámabók* was variously the grandson or great-grandson of Hrómundr.[6]

The saga of Hrómundr Gripsson allegedly told at the wedding-feast at Reykjahólar is now lost. But a sequence of verses survives called *Griplur,* based on the saga, perhaps composed soon after the mid-fourteenth century.[7] The saga printed in *Fornaldarsögur Norðurlanda* is said to be based on these verses.[8]

Griplur tells of Hrómundr's expedition south to France (Valland) and of how he broke into the mound of Þráinn. The mound-dweller is described as sitting on his throne "with the aspect of no man"

---

3 Brown 1952, ix-xxix. Foote 1984, 65-76 and works referred to there.
4 von See 1981, 91-95. Foote 1984, 76-83.
5 Jesch 1984, 89-105.
6 *Landnámabók* 1968, 38-40, note 1 and works referred to there.
7 Björn K. Þórólfsson 1934, 353-63. See further Ólafur Halldórsson in *KLNM* XIV 1969, 319-23 and works referred to there.
8 *Fornaldarsögur Norðurlanda* II, 271-286.

(*ásjón einskis manns*) but "swollen" (*bólginn*) and "black as hell" (*blár sem hel*) while he kindled fire under a cauldron between his knees full of dead bodies. Hrómundr took possession of Þráinn's gold and treasure and provoked him to come to grips with him, as the verses describe:

> Gripsson lítur garpinn blá,
> gengr í móti draugi,
> rennaz til ok ráðaz á
> rammir tveir í haugi.
>
> Skrykkjum gengur skáli flagðs,
> skelfur allt í næri;
> það mun kenna kempu bragðs
> að koma við Þráin í færi.
>
> Gripsson lætur grjót og tré
> ganga upp hinn mæti,
> þá varð leiðr að lúta á kné
> loddarinn öðrum fæti.[9]

(Gripsson looks upon the black fellow, approaches the ghost; those two mighty ones hurtle together and come to grips in the mound. The hall of the evil monster is in tumult; all around shakes; it may be recorded as a champion's deed to come to grips with Þráinn. The noble Gripsson sends flying both stone and wood; the hideous churl was forced to go down on one knee.)

The verses go on to describe how Þráinn attacked Hrómundr with his nails and tore the flesh from the bone. As they wrestled, they spouted verses at each other. Hrómundr finally succeeded in bringing Þráinn down with a wrestling-feint. Now he also made use of Þráinn's sword Mistilteinn to cut off the mound-dweller's head, then lit a fire and burnt him up, and came out of the mound.[10]

The account of the wrestling of Hrómundr and Þráinn is much the same in *Hrómundar saga Gripssonar*, and there the description of the ghost/mound-dweller is similar.[11]

---

9 *Rímnasafn* I 1905-12, 37-38. About the word *loddari,* see Gunnell 1995, 360-362.
10 *Rímnasafn* I, 37-58.
11 *Fornaldarsögur Norðurlanda* II 1944, 276-278.

The oldest written source in which a living man struggles with the dead in his mound is Saxo's description (soon after 1200) of Ásmundr wrestling with the dead Ásviðr. Ásviðr died in his sickbed, and Ásmundr had himself buried in the mound beside him, together with some provisions. When the mound was opened soon after, Ásmundr appeared, his face covered with blood. Ásviðr had come to life every night, wrestled with Ásmundr and torn off his left ear. Ásmundr described their struggles:

> ... contra exanimem conserui vim,
> Grave luctæ subiens pondus et immane periclum.
> Laceris unguibus in me redivivus ruit Asuit,
> Stygia vi reparans post cineres horrida bella.
> ...
> Nescio quo stygii numinis ausu
> Missus ab inferis spiritus Asuit
> Sævis alipedem dentibus edit,
> Infandoque canem præbuit ori.
> Nec contentus equi vel canis esu,
> Mox in me rapidos transtulit ungues,
> Discissaque gena sustilit aurem.
> Hinc laceri vultus horret imago,
> Emicat inque fero vulnere sanguis.
> Haud impune tamen monstrifer egit;
> Nam ferro secui mox caput ejus,
> Perfodique nocens stipite corpus.[12]

> (... I have struggled against a phantom's energi,
> wrestled with grievious strain and immense peril. Asvith
> returned from the other world with ghostly violence; his gashing
> nails attacked me, renewing fierce battle after his death.
> ...
> By some piece of hellish daring
> Asvith's spirit was launched from the shades
> with ferocious teeth to devour the steed
> and lift the dog to its monstrous jaws.
> But horse nor dog sated its hunger;
> swiftly it turned its lightning talons
> to slash my cheek and take off my ear.

---

12 Saxonis Grammatici 1859, 245-246.

Hence the ghostly sight of my torn
visage, where blood wells from the cruel
wound. Yet the ghoul did not go unscathed;
I was quick to scythe off its head with my sword
and thrust a stake through its wicked body. [13]

In *Grettis saga*, assigned to the early fourteenth century, [14] it is related that Grettir entered the mound of Kárr the Old on the island of Haramsøy off the coast of Norway. Auðunn held the rope for him. When Grettir had collected everything that he found of value in the mound, the story says:

> ... ok er hann gekk útar eptir hauginum, var gripit til hans fast. Lét hann þá laust féit, en rézk í mót þeim, ok tókusk þeir þá til heldr óþyrmiliga. Gekk nú upp allt þat, er fyrir varð; sótti haug-búinn með kappi. Grettir fór undan lengi, en þar kemr, at hann sér, at eigi muni duga at hlífask við. Sparir nú hvárrgi annan; færask þeir þangat, er hestbeinin váru; kippðusk þeir þar um lengi, ok fóru ýmsir á kné, en svá lauk, at haugbúinn féll á bak aptr, ok varð af því dykr mikill. Þá hljóp Auðunn frá festarhaldinu ok ætlaði, at Grettir myndi dauðr. Grettir brá nú sverðinu Jǫkulsnaut ok hjó á háls haugbúanum, svá at af tók hǫfuðit; setti hann það við þjó honum. Gekk hann síðan til festar með féit,... [15]

(... as he went round the outer edge of the mound, something reached out and took a firm grasp at him. Then he let go of the treasure and attacked the thing so they wrestled together some-what roughly. Everything in sight went flying; the mound-dweller attacked vigorously. Grettir gave way for a long time, but it came to the point when he saw that holding back would not do. Neither gave quarter; they reached a place where a horse's bones were lying; they struggled long against each other, now one and now the other coming down, and finally the mound-dweller fell

---

13 Saxo Grammaticus 1979, 151. In his commentary on the translation, John Fisher says: "Saxo in referring to the dead Asvith has *exanimem vim* (a dead man's force). My trans-lation of 'phantom' may be slightly misleading, since Saxo may be thinking of an ani-mated corpse" (Saxo Grammaticus 1980, 88). This view can be seconded. See further Saxo Grammaticus 1985, 190-92, and *Fornaldarsögur Norðurlanda* III, 166.
14 Björn Sigfússon in *KLNM* 1960, 460-61 and works cited there. See further Óskar Halldórsson 1982, 5-36.
15 *ÍF* VII, 58.

backwards with a resounding crash. Then Auðunn left his place by
the rope, thinking that Grettir must be dead. Grettir now drew
his sword Jǫkulsnaut and struck the neck of the mound-dweller so
as to sever his head; he put it beside the thigh. Next he went
towards the rope with the treasure...)

In *Harðar saga ok Hólmverja*, dated to the fourteenth century, it is
told how Hǫrðr and Geir entered the mound of Sóti in Gautland in
Sweden. Sóti is described as "fearsome", and when Hǫrðr made as if
to steal the treasure in the mound, a struggle ensued:

Þá spratt Sóti upp ok rann á Hǫrð. Varð þar harðr atgangr, þess at
Hǫrðr varð mjǫk aflvani. Tók Sóti svá fast, at hold Harðar hljóp
saman í hnykla. Hǫrðr bað Geir tendra vaxkertit ok vita, hve Sóta
brygði við þat. En er ljósit bar yfir Sóta, ómætti hann, ok fell hann
niðr.[16]

(Then Sóti sprang up and ran at Hǫrðr. The resulting struggle was
so fierce that Hǫrðr was much exhausted. Sóti took such a firm
hold that Hǫrðr's flesh ran together in lumps. Hǫrðr told Geirr to
light a wax candle and see how Sóti would take that. And when
the light reached Sóti he lost all power and fell down.)

Hǫrðr and Sóti were spouting verses at each other throughout
the struggle; but when Hǫrðr asked Geirr to bring up the candle
the ghost plunged into the earth and disappeared.[17]

The account in *Grettis saga* of Grettir wrestling with Kárr is in
ch. 18. In ch. 35 we hear of Grettir's other wrestling match with the
ghost of Glámr, a struggle that took place in Iceland, at Þórhalla-
staðir in Forsæludalur. It began by Grettir and Glámr pulling
against each other for Grettir's cloak. Next:

... kippðu nú í sundur feldinum í millum sín... Ok í því hljóp
Grettir undir hendr honum ok þreif um hann miðjan ok spennti á
honum hrygginn sem fastast gat hann, ok ætlaði at Glámr skyldi
kikna við; en þrællinn lagði at handleggjum Grettis svá fast, at
hann hǫrfaði allr fyrir orku sakar. Fór Grettir þá undan í ýmis
setin; gengu þá frá stokkarnir, ok allt brotnaði, þat er fyrir varð.

16 *ÍF* XIII 1991, 42.
17 Ibid, 43.

Vildi Glámr leita út, en Grettir færði við fætr, hvar sem hann mátti, en þó gat Glámr dregit hann fram úr skálanum. Áttu þeir þá allharða sókn, því at þrællinn ætlaði at koma honum út úr bænum; en svá illt, sem at eiga var við Glám inni, þá sá Grettir, at þó var verra at fásk við hann úti, ok því brauzk hann í móti af ǫllu afli at fara út. Glámr færðisk í aukana ok kneppði hann at sér, er þeir kómu í anddyrit. Ok er Grettir sér, at hann fekk eigi við spornat, hefir hann allt eitt atriðit at hann hleypr sem harðask í fang þrælnum ok spyrnir báðum fótum í jarðfastan stein, er stóð í durunum. Við þessu bjósk þrællinn eigi; hann hafði þá togazk við at draga Gretti at sér, ok því kiknaði Glámr á bak aptr ok rauk ǫfugr út á dyrrnar, svá at herðarnar námu uppdyrit, ok ræfrit gekk í sundr, bæði viðirnir ok þekjan frǫrin; fell hann svá opinn ok ǫfugr út úr húsunum, en Grettir á hann ofan.[18]

(... they tore the cloak apart between them... and thereupon Grettir seized him under the arms and grasped him round the middle as hard as he could, expecting Glámr to sink down; but the thrall put such a grip on Grettir's arm that he gave way under the force of it. Grettir then retreated from one seat to another; the beams were dislodged and everything in their path was smashed. Glámr was bent on getting out, while Grettir set his feet against anything he could find; yet Glámr was able to drag him out of the hall. They had a fierce struggle, for the thrall meant to get him out of the building. Now Grettir saw that hard as it was to tackle Glámr indoors, it was still worse to deal with him outside; so he resisted going out with all his might. Glámr had an access of strength, and clutched Grettir to him as they got into the porch. When Grettir saw that he could not hold his ground, he simultaneously flung himself with great force upon the thrall's breast and rammed both feet against a stone set in the ground at the doorway. The thrall was taken by surprise; he had been pulling to drag Grettir towards himself, and now he sank down on his knees and fell backwards through the door-frame, so that his shoulders hit the lintel and the roof was torn apart, both timbers and frozen thatch; thus he fell up and backwards out of the building, with Grettir on top of him.)

As Glámr fell, he shot a piercing glance at Grettir so that he was helpless for a time, while Glámr recited imprecations against him. But as soon as the faintness passed, Grettir struck off Glámr's head

---

18 *ÍF* VII 1936, 120-121.

and laid it beside his thigh. The farmer now came up and thanked Grettir for overcoming this "unclean spirit (*óhreina anda*)", and together they burnt Glámr and buried the ashes.[19]

The stories quoted here show that the narrative motif of wrestling with a ghost or revenant was widespread in the Nordic countries from the twelfth to fourteenth centuries.[20] It seems mostly to be a matter of breaking into a mound and wrestling with the mound-dweller (Þráinn, Ásviðr, Sóti, Kárr); but struggles with revenants are not confined to mounds (Glámr). In these stories the dead man always appears in the flesh, ghosts take food (Þráinn, Ásviðr and perhaps Kárr, cf. the horse-bones), their onslaughts are endowed with superhuman power, and sometimes they scratch opponents with their nails (Þráinn, Ásviðr). When the ghosts are successfully overcome, the head is commonly cut off (Þráinn, Ásviðr, Kárr, Glámr) and sometimes placed beside the thigh (Kárr, Glámr). Finally the ghost is burnt up (Þráinn, Glámr). Sóti is exceptional in that he disappeared into the ground before the usual methods could be applied.

A feature shared by all these stories is that they are located far away from the place where they were recorded or allegedly reported. More often than not it is a distance of both time and space; this applies to all stories of mound-breaking. The story of the wrestling of Grettir and Glámr was written down some three hundred years after the struggles were supposed to have taken place. Thus it is risky to assume that the writers or narrators expected readers or hearers to believe these tales. In *Þorgils saga ok Hafliða* it is stated outright that the account of Hrómundr's wrestling with Þráinn was an untrue story, even though Hrómundr himself was a historic person. It may be predicted that the rest of the medieval stories were looked upon in much the same way.

II

Shortly before the turn of the last century, tales were current in the Western Fjords of Iceland about a ghost endowed with supernatural

---

19 Ibid., 122.
20 On the question of the wider circulation of this motif, see Davidson 1981, 155-175.

power at a farm called Bæir. This ghost reputedly attacked two young men of the district. Traditions of these events are recorded in three collections of Icelandic folklore. Two versions have similar accounts, for they rely in large part of the same informants, but there is real divergence in the third version. I refer here to one of the two first-mentioned versions, in *Vestfirzkar sagnir* collected by Arngrímur Fr. Bjarnason. This account is recorded by Kolbeinn Jakobsson, the farmer at Unaðsdalur, the next farm to Bæir. He relates, among other matters, a conversation he had with Rósinkar, one of the two attacked, fourteen days after the events described took place. This young man told Kolbeinn and the parish priest that on 12 December 1892 he had walked a few minutes' distance between farm buildings in the dark when some kind of being came towards him, which "... mér sýndist manni líkt, en höfuðið þó öðruvísi"[21] ("seemed to me like a man, but the head was different"). Rósinkar made several efforts to get past this being, so he said, but without success. The story goes on:

> Skipti það engum togum, er ég hljóp á brautina, að þetta – er ég þá glögglega sá, að var maður með höndum og fótum og höfði að öðru leyti en því, að andlitið vantaði, – greip í mig að aftanverðu. Sneri ég mér þá snöggt að þessum ófagnaði, hugðist geta tekið hann föstum tökum, sem ég þó alls ekki gat, því mér fannst hann sem hvelja eða lopi að taka á; hins vegar fannst mér þetta klípa mig svo sem hold gengi frá beinum... Er við komum að sundinu, sleppti ókind þessi tökum á mér, en greip í stað þess í trefil minn... toguðumst við á um hann í sundinu unz trefillinn slitnaði, eða þetta sleppti honum; veit ekki hvort heldur var, – Hrökk ég þá um leið aftur á bak niður á bæjarhlaðið, gat þó fótað mig, og náð í skúrardyr að inngangi í bæinn, komst inn og upp á baðstofuloftið, og hné þá í ómegin.[22]

> (As soon as I reached the path, the thing – which I saw plainly to be a man with hands and feet and head, apart from the fact that the face was missing – seized me from behind. I turned suddenly on this gruesome thing, meaning to take a fast hold of it, which I could not do at all, since it seemed like a fish-skin or limp flesh to the touch. On the other hand, I felt it nipping me so as to pull my

21 *Vestfirzkar sagnir* III 1946, 4.
22 Ibid., 5.

flesh from my bones... when we came to the passage-way the nasty creature loosed hold of me, but seized my muffler instead... we tugged at it in the passage-way until the muffler tore apart, or he lost hold of it, I don't know which. I fell down backwards on the paving round the farmstead, but regained my footing and reached the porch at the entry, got in and up to the sitting-room floor, then fainted away.)

The priest said this would have been a seal but Rósinkar firmly contradicted, saying it had been just as he described. These attacks continued over the New Year, and Rósinkar died between January and February. He was bedridden for the last few weeks "prostrated by terror and loss of nerve", so that a light was kept burning beside him and the dormer window over his bed was closely blocked.[23]

Kolbeinn next describes in his narrative how a friend of Rósinkar's, Benedikt Brynjólfsson (Bensi) was subject to attacks by this same ghost after the death of Rósinkar. It was said that Benedikt had provoked the ghost to come to grips, with the following results:

> "Er ég kom hérna upp á Bæjahjallann, kom þessi svo kallaði draugur, sem mun hafa ráðið niðurlögum Rósinkars sálaða, á móti mér, tókst á við mig, reif föt mín og hrinti mér undan sér niður fyrir hjallann, og allt þangað til ég, eftir illan leik, komst hér inn í bæinn." Sýndi María mér þá strigafataræfla þá, er Bensi sagði að draugurinn hefði rifið.[24]

> ("When I was at the ridge here at Bæir, this so-called ghost, which will have caused the downfall of the late Rósinkar, attacked me, wrestled with me, tore my clothes and pushed me ahead down from the ridge to the point where I got into the farm here with great difficulty." María showed me the ragged strip of cloth which Bensi said the ghost had torn.)

Páll Halldórsson, María's son, on the same occasion told Kolbeinn what happened next day, when he and Benedikt were feeding the animals:

---

23 Ibid., 6-7.
24 Ibid., 8.

"... sá að verið var að henda Bensa aftur og fram eftir þúfunum undir hólbrekkunni. Var þá Bensi naumast orðinn sjálfbjarga, svo ég varð að hjálpa honum í bæinn; sagði hann svo frá: að þegar hann hefði komið inn í fjárhúsið, en skilið eftir opnar dyrnar, og ætlað að taka moðpokann úr jötunni, þá hefði draugsi komið inn, keyrt sig aftur á bak, dregið sig út úr húsinu og niður fyrir hól-brekkuna, og hent sér eftir þúfunum, svo að hann hefði engri vörn getað fyrir sig komið."[25]

("I saw that Bensi was being tossed to and fro across the knolls under the slope of the hillock. Bensi was by then scarcely in con-trol of himself, so that I had to help him into the farm. This is what he told me: as soon as he got into the byre, leaving the door open, and was about to take the chaff-sack from the manger, in came the ghost, which thrust him backwards, dragged him out of the building and down over the slopes of the hillock and tossed him to and fro across the knolls, so that he could not put up any defence.")

After this Benedikt did not dare go out alone after dusk while he was at Bæir, according to the account of Páll and María.

Not everyone was convinced that Bensi was telling the truth about his encounter with the ghost. One of the doubters was his father Brynjólfur. So he went out of his way to investigate the mat-ter, and a little while later he said: "Now I will no longer say that my son Bensi is lying."[26]

The account of Kolbeinn by Unaðsdalur contains an explanation of these hauntings by Guðrún Jónsdóttir, sister-in-law of Kolbeinn and aunt of Rósinkar. She stated that she was present when Rósin-kar got into a fight with a man called Bjarni at a fishing-station in the spring of 1892. Rósinkar had got Bjarni down and treated him roughly. Then Bjarni said, according to Guðrún: "Though you have been able to get me down this time, some time or other I will get you down, if not during my lifetime, then after death." These threats were coupled with the most terrible oaths, according to Guðrún. Kolbeinn said that he would have had no more faith in this story of revenge than in any other such, if Bjarni had not died just

---

25 Ibid., 9.
26 Ibid., 10-11.

when the hauntings began. By making enquiries, he discovered that Bjarni drowned in a shipwreck on 12 December 1892, the same day that the hauntings at Bæir began.[27]

The account given by Kolbeinn of Unaðsdalur of the hauntings at Bæir is exceptional in that Kolbeinn lived in the immediate neighbourhood of Bæir, and made detailed inquiries into the events very soon after they were said to have happened. Then Kolbeinn also stresses in the course of his narrative that he had very little faith in supernatural events, admitting at the same time that he could not find any natural explanation for what was going on.[28]

The two other accounts of the ghost of Bæir have in common a greater distance from the scene of events. The narrative is far more polished, the struggle of Rósinkar with the evil thing is a matter of life and death, and additional motifs are introduced which are not found in the version of Kolbeinn of Unaðsdalur. Both of these accounts attribute the onset of the hauntings to the fact that Rósinkar and Benedikt found the body of a drowned man in the autumn of 1892. *Gráskinna hin meiri* says:

> Líkið var illa útlítandi og lagði af því megna fýlu... Þeir ráðast báðir að líkinu og ýta því frá landi með óhljóðum og illum munn-söfnuði. Skiljast þeir ekki fyrr við hinn dauða en þeir standa upp í mitti í sjó og stjaka honum eins langt út og þeir náðu til hans með göngustöfunum.[29]

> (The body was in bad condition and gave off a strong stench... They both set upon the body and pushed it away from land with rude shouts and foul language. They did not leave the dead man until they were waist-high in the sea, shoving him out as far as they could with walking staffs.)

In the third account, printed in Guðni Jónsson's *Íslenzkir sagna-þættir og þjóðsögur*, it is added that the body washed up was that of a contemporary and comrade of Rósinkar and Benedikt. According to this source, they had previously ill-treated their comrade Jón, and

---

27 Ibid., 11-14.
28 Ibid., 6, 12. Cf. various articles in *Folklore of Ghosts* 1981, specially 109 ff. and 155 ff..
29 *Gráskinna hin meiri* I 1962, 332.

he had threatened them. When they were on their way home after having abused his body, the story goes:

> ... mæta þeir Jóni enn, og er hann nú ekki lengur að velkjast í sjónum, heldur kominn á þurrt land og uppistandandi og er nú afturgenginn og lætur allt annað en friðlega... Kastar hann að þeim bæði snjó og grjóti... Eigi fengu þeir betur séð en að draugurinn tætti upp gaddaða jörðina... Komust þeir loks í vökulok heim að Bæjum, allir rifnir og tættir, særðir og blóðugir og þrekaðir mjög og Rósinkar viti sínu fjær af ofraun og skelfingu.[30]

> (... they met Jón again, and now he was no longer tossing on the sea, but had reached dry land and was standing upright; now he was a corpse revived and looked far from genial... He threw both snow and stones at them... it looked to them just as if the ghost was tearing up hard-frozen earth... Finally they reached Bæir at bedtime, all tattered and torn, hurt and bleeding and dead-tired; Rósinkar was out of his mind with exhaustion and terror.)

The descriptions of the above narrative are not unlike those in the account of Þráinn and the story of Glámr which I have discussed above. It is proper to stress that the story of the finding of the body appears to be a later addition, since the informants closest to the events, three in all, state that Benedikt denied that he had found a body.[31]

In the collection published by Magnús Gestsson, *Úr vesturbyggðum Barðastrandasýslu,* a story called "Einhenti draugurinn", ("The One-armed Ghost") is printed. The tale is about Hjalti Þorgeirson (d. 1917), who was in his youth a person of tremendous strength. He wrestled with a man and handled him very roughly, and the other flew into a rage and vowed to get his own back, alive or dead. Many years later, Hjalti was attacked when he was out and about before dawn:

> ... verða átök löng og hörð og þykir Hjalta tvísýnt um úrslit... Rennur nú berserksgangur á Hjalta og tekst honum að lokum að vinna bug á andstæðingnum... Hjalti kom heim þegar liðið var á

---

30 *Íslenzkir sagnaþættir og þjóðsögur* XII 1957, 22.
31 *Gráskinna hin meiri* 1962, 333.

morgun og var þrekaður mjög og föt hans rifin... sagði hann, að sá sem á hann réðst hefði verið hinn sami og forðum hefði heitast við sig... Hefði hann nú verið stórum verri viðskiptis en í fyrra skiptið, en það hefði viljað sér til lífs, að á hann hefði nú vantað annan handlegginn.[32]

(... the struggle was long and hard, and Hjalti saw that the outcome was doubtful... He had an access of berserk fury and finally managed to get the better of his adversary... Hjalti reached home late in the morning, much exhausted and with his clothes torn... He said that his attacker was the same man who had threatened him years before. He had now become a much more dangerous customer than before; but one of his arms was missing, and this was why Hjalti escaped with his life.)

The story later tells that the body of a big man was washed up, one arm being missing. It was buried as the law requires, and Hjalti attended the funeral. Then, it says:

... biður Hjalti grafarmennina að doka... bregður sér nú bak við kirkjuna og kemur aftur með stein einn mikinn... Lætur hann steinhellu þessa þversum ofan á kistuna og segir um leið, að hann vonist til að þetta dugi til að maðurinn liggi kyrr þar sem hann er kominn.[33]

(... Hjalti asked the bearers to wait a little... then he made off behind the church and returned with a large slab of rock... He placed this slab across the coffin, saying as he did so that he hoped this would make sure that the fellow lay still where he was put.)

Essentially the same way of thinking underlies this story as that found in the story of the Ghost of Bæir. The events also resemble those in the alternative explanation of the origin of the ghost. A man who had threatened to avenge himself dead if not alive would be likely to keep his word, according to the prevalent folk-belief.[34] The story of Hjalti also makes plain the close connection between the revenant and his body; and this calls to mind the variant version of "The Ghost of Bæir", where the two friends abuse a corpse cast up

---

32 Magnús Gestsson 1973, 142-143.
33 Ibid., 143.
34 Jón Árnason VI 1961, 280; *heitingar* and references.

by the sea which almost at once begins its hauntings. The ghost that wrestled with Hjalti lacked one arm, and an arm had broken off from the body washed up soon after. Hjalti's procedure in the churchyard is notable, not least because it recalls a parallel practice described as occurring in Greenland in the Middle Ages.[35] Thus it seems as if a traditional motif which occurs in medieval Icelandic literature was alive and kicking in folklore accounts current in Iceland in the nineteenth century and even later.

It is natural enough that stories of wrestling with a ghost or dead man should be influenced by a conventional motif which has survived in this country for centuries on end. And this conventional motif must prompt particular caution when we evaluate stories like "The Ghost of Bæir" and "Hjalti and the One-armed Ghost". People who were allegedly exposed to this actual or imagined trial were sometimes out alone, and therefore the only ones to tell the tale. It could have been tempting to represent encounters, which possibly did them no credit and led to unpleasant results and torn clothes, as wrestling with a ghost. The procedure of Hjalti in the churchyard could then be an episode in the denouement of a drama of this sort. On the other hand, the story of the encounter of Rósinkar and Benedikt with the ghost of Bæir cannot be called in question on these grounds. Rósinkar fainted away when he got into the farm after his first encounter with the ghost, and he told of the incident soon after to the man who recorded it. This same man could also rely on the account of an eye-witness as to how Benedikt was flung to and fro. Both the eye-witness and the man who wrote down the story were most reluctant to believe that any superhuman agency was concerned. Thus everything tends towards the conclusion that something happened at Bæir that was not to be explained in natural terms. And it is a fact that Rósinkar died because of some actual or imagined attacks.

III

When we try to answer the question of what made people believe in good faith that they or others round them had wrestled with a ghost or revenant, the first step is to look at some episodes in Icelandic

35 Nørlund 1972, 48. Cf. *ÍF* VI, 56.

folk-tales. In the *Þjóðsögur* of Jón Árnason there is a short tale entitled "Skorravíkur-Jón", ("Jón of Skorravík"). The subject is a trip
by boat of Jón with his daughter and a certain Guðmundur. The
boat overturned. The story continues:

> Dóttir hans drukknaði... en Guðmundur komst á kjöl og gat
> haldið sér þar. Jón var syndur og greip í fótinn á Guðmundi...
> Guðmundur var röskur maður og vildi verja líf sitt og sparkaði
> hann svo hart til Jóns með fætinum að hann sökk. En er Guð-
> mundi skolaði á land sá hann Jón þar afturgenginn og réðst hann
> þegar á Guðmund.[36]
>
> (The daughter drowned... but Guðmundur got onto the keel and
> managed to keep his position. Jón could swim, and he grabbed at
> Guðmundur's foot... Guðmundur, being a vigorous man and
> wanting to save his life, gave Jón such a kick that he sank. But
> when Guðmundur was washed ashore he saw Jón haunting it, and
> he immediately attacked Guðmundur.)

The story tells no more of their encounter, but evidently Guðmundur got the upper hand. That same evening people went down
to the shore:

> Fundu þeir þá Guðmund og lá hann í ómegi; augun voru öll
> blóðhlaupin og búkurinn allur marinn. Langt leið áður en hann
> gat þolað að horfa í dagsbirtuna og hryllti jafnan við er hann min-
> ntist á þennan óttalega atburð. Sagan er tekin eftir kvenmanni sem
> Guðmundur hafði sjálfur sagt hana oftar en einu sinni.[37]
>
> (There they found Guðmundur lying senseless; his eyes were heav-
> ily bloodshot and his trunk badly bruised. It was a long time
> before he could bear the light of day, and he always shuddered at
> the memory of this frightful incident. The story is taken from a
> woman who heard it time and again from Guðmundur himself.)

The most natural explanation of this story seems to me that Jón
reached land alive. We can leave it an open question whether Guðmundur believed that Jón had come back to life, or whether he saw
it to his advantage to tell of wrestling with a ghost and overcoming

---

36 Jón Árnason I 1961, 247.
37 Ibid.

it, rather than admit that he had struggled with a man and killed
him. But the people who told the story, and those who wrote it
down and found room for it among folk-tales all judged that Jón
was a revenant when he wrestled with Guðmundur.[38]

In the *Þjóðsögur og sagnir* of Sigfús Sigfússon there is a tale which
is still more transparent than the tale of Jón of Skorravík. It is entitled "Afturganga?" ("A Haunting?"), and the question mark shows
that the writer was not altogether sure of his ground. The story tells
of a man who fell ill and died. A man called Bjarni, a carpenter and
a stout fellow, had to make the coffin. Intending to measure the
body, he went with a maidservant to the shed where the body lay:

> Þegar þau komu í skemmuna sat sá framliðni uppi réttum beinum
> á líkbörunum. Bjarni lofar guð fyrir lífgjöf hans og ætlar að hon-
> um. En hinn ræðst þegar á Bjarna af miklu afli. Takast nú harðar
> sviptingar því Bjarni var heljarmenni. Stúlkan hljóp inn að sækja
> mannhjálp og skildi ljósið eftir á gólfinu. Þegar karlar komu aftur
> með stúlkunni hneig hinn framliðni máttvana á gólfið og lögðu
> þeir hann aftur á líkbörurnar.[39]

> (As they entered the shed, the dead man was sitting on the bier
> with legs outstretched. Bjarni thanks God for his recovery, and
> makes to approach him. But the other straightway attacks Bjarni
> in full strength. A fierce struggle ensues, for Bjarni was a man of
> gigantic strength. The girl rushed off to seek help, leaving the
> lamp on the floor. When she returned with the menfolk the dead
> man had fallen powerless on the floor, and they put him back on
> the bier.)

The events related in this story must have taken place in about
1840, but the story itself was recorded about the turn of the last
century. Bjarni's grandsons are named as contemporaries of the person who recorded it, and it is expressly stated that he and his sons
had all been well liked.

This last story displays better than most the strong pull of folk-
belief that preserves stories of wrestling with a ghost. In Icelandic

---

38 The story is placed among tales of revenants and dead men who have a grudge against
the living.

39 Sigfús Sigfússon III 1982, 121.

folk-lore collections there are many such stories telling of similar events, and there are other passages which strongly indicate that the fear of a man not quite dead haunting the place led to his summary despatch. I give one example here.

In the *Þjóðsögur* of Jón Árnason, the *Þjóðsögur og sagnir* of Sigfús Sigfússon, and elsewhere there is the story of Bjarna-Dísa, Þórdís, who was left behind in a hollowed snowdrift on Fjarðarheiði by her brother Bjarni in the year 1797. When they came to find her she was alive and speaking; those who found her assumed she was a revenant. One of them, called Þorvaldur, a man of great strength, attacked her and put an end to her. In the account of this in the *Þjóðsögur og sagnir* of Sigfús Sigfússon we can see the popular belief at the turn of the century, for it is said:

> Ætla það flestir vantrúaðir menn nú á dögum að Dísa hafi haldið lífinu... Þorvaldur hafi drepið hana í oftrúaræði sínu. En þeir sem þekkja afreksverk hennar eftir dauðann sætta sig við hitt sem áður segir að hún hafi þarna gengið aftur hálfum afturgangi.[40]

> (Most unbelieving people these days suppose that Dísa was still alive... and that Þorvaldur killed her in the fervour of his excessive belief. But those who know of her prowess after death are content with the opposite view stated above, that she was haunting the place as a half-revenant.)

In this story "half-revenant" refers to the fact that Dísa had twice but not three times jumped around in her wretched lair; or from the standing position (Jón Árnason). Also, she had uttered only two cries, not the third. Þorvaldur saw the urgency of preventing her from haunting as a full revenant, according to the story.

The tale of Skorravíkur-Jón, the man who sat up on the bier, and that of Bjarna-Dísa seem to show that a live person was killed because of belief in hauntings. Thus these examples support the conclusion that people believed that those recently dead could come back as ghosts in physical form. So it is quite credible that actual events could in some way spark off stories about wrestling with a ghost or a dead man come back to life.

---

40 Ibid., 164-181, and works cited there.

IV

Finally, it is as well to summarise briefly what can be deduced from the samples given above.

1. Tales were current in the twelfth, thirteenth and fourteenth centuries about a hero wrestling with ghosts, mound-dwellers or revenants. The mound-dweller story appears to be the oldest and most primitive, influencing later stories such as the struggle between Grettir and Glámr.

2. *Grettis saga* was one of the best-loved of the Icelandic sagas, and the story of the struggle between Glámr and Grettir has lived on in Iceland throughout the ages. It was in a position to set its impress on stories of dealings with ghosts which arose at later periods.

3. Towards the turn of the last century, stories came into circulation about the struggle of two young men with a ghost at Bæir on Snæfjallaströnd; a reliable contemporary witness goes to show that something was going on which cannot be explained in natural terms.

4. Later accounts of the events at Bæir show that these tales rapidly fell into a pattern similar to the one found in *Grettis saga* and other ancient tellings of struggle with dead men.

5. In some folk-tales and stories of the nineteenth and twentieth centuries there are indications that belief in the ability of the newly dead to haunt led to the killing of people still alive.

Translated by Joan Turville-Petre

*This article is a slightly edited version of a paper given at University College Dublin, in March 1984 and at the 8th Congress of the International Society for Folk Narrative Research, Bergen, Norway, June 12th-17th 1984. Originally published in *Arv, Scandinavian Yearbook of Folklore* Vol. 43. 1987.

Ágrip

Glíman við drauginn

GLÍMAN við drauginn á sér fornar rætur í íslenskri sagnahefð. Samkvæmt *Þorgils sögu og Hafliða* sem talin er rituð á fyrstu áratugum 13. aldar var gestum í brúðkaupinu á Reykjahólum árið 1119 skemmt með frásögn af því er Hrómundur Gripsson braust inn í haug Þráins og glímdi við drauginn. Er hörðum átökum þeirra lýst fjálglega í rímum af Hrómundi sem greina frá því hvernig hann yfirvann drauginn að lokum með harðfylgi, hjó af honum höfuðið, brenndi hann til ösku og fór síðan úr hauginum.

Í *Danmerkursögu* Saxa frá því um 1200 segir frá glímu Ásmundar við Ásvið dauðan í haugi. Sama minni kemur fyrir í *Grettis sögu* er Grettir fór í haug Kárs og rændi hann sverði. Bæði Ásmundur og Grettir höfðu sama hátt á og Hrómundur þegar þeir höfðu fellt andstæðinginn. Þeir hjuggu af draugnum höfuðið. Þeirri aðgerð gat Hörður hins vegar ekki komið við í haugi Sóta sem hvarf í jörð niður. Gretti tókst eftir harða glímu að höggva höfuðið af Glámi, sem þó er kallaður óhreinn andi í sögunni.

Í *Þorgils sögu og Hafliða* er skýrt tekið fram, að frásögnin af glímu Hrómundar við Þráin sé lygasaga. Má ætla að svipaðs viðhorfs hafi gætt á miðöldum til annarra sagna um glímuna við drauginn sem hér hafa verið raktar.

Grettis saga var ætíð í hópi vinsælustu Íslandingasagna og frásögn sögunnar af glímu Grettis við Glám mótaði í ríkum mæli sagnamyndun á síðari öldum þegar upp kom minnið um glímuna við drauginn.

Laust fyrir síðustu aldamót komst á kreik saga á Bæjum á Snæfjallaströnd af glímu tveggja ungra manna við draug. Samkvæmt frásögn trúverðugra sögumanna sem urðu vitni að atburðum virðist þar hafa verið um að ræða fyrirbæri sem torvelt er að skýra að náttúrulegum hætti. Sagnamyndun af þessum atburðum féll hins vegar snemma í farveg sem minnti um margt á frásögn *Grettis sögu* af glímunni við Glám og hliðstæðar fornar sagnir um glímu lifandi manna við afturgengna.

Í þjóðsögum og sögnum frá nítjándu öld um glímuna við drauginn virðist stundum hafa verið um að ræða fólk sem hafði verið talið látið en vaknaði til lífsins. Nærstaddir héldu að um afturgöngu væri að ræða og einhver hetjan réðist á lifandi manneskjuna og gerði út af við hana.

The Ghost that Wrestled with Guðmundur

THE FOLLOWING CHAPTER contains a further three tales about wrestling with ghosts which come from eastern Iceland. All of them were recorded about, or shortly after the middle of the twentieth century, but to my mind they may well shed new light on some of the examples that have been discussed earlier in this volume.[1]

In his book *Af Jökulsmönnum og fleira fólki,* Þorkell Björnsson from Hnefilsdalur, has published the following account which bears the title "Glímt við draug" ("Wrestling with a Ghost"):

Maður einn, sem var vinnumaður á Skeggjastöðum, lenti eitt sinn í hörkuáflogum við draug. Held ég, að enginn viti enn þann dag í dag, hvað þar var á ferðinni. Vinnumaður þessi hét Guðmundur, ég hygg Jónsson, kenndur við Krossavík og var hann heljarmenni að burðum.

Þegar þetta bar til, var hann gangandi. Prentuð heimild segir frá því, að þegar hann var að fara yfir Heiðarendann frá Heiðarseli og norður fyrir, hafi hann séð einhvern á hlið við sig alla tíð. En móðir mín og afi sögðu mér þannig frá, að þegar Guðmundur var kominn inn fyrir Teigasel, byrjaður síðustu bæjarleiðina, hafi hann orðið draugsa var í lænu, rétt innan við Teigarána, fyrir innan Teigasel. Draugsi kom þar niður lænuna, sem síðan er kölluð Draugslág. Draugurinn þvældist svo fyrir Guðmundi sitt á hvað lengstaf alla leiðina heim. Þetta endaði með því, að þeir Guðmundur og draugurinn flugust á síðasta hluta leiðarinnar. Guðmundur dróst svo heim mjög illa til reika, með fötin sundurtætt og hálsinn bláan og marinn. Hann var rúmliggjandi næstu daga. Því má svo við bæta, að afi minn sagði mér svo frá, að eftir þetta hefði hann þurft að fylgja Guðmundi til gegninganna í lambhúsin, það sem eftir var vetrar, vegna myrkfælni hans.[2]

1   See previous article.
2   Þorkell Björnson 1981, 127.

(There was a labourer at Skeggjastaðir who once got caught up in a fight with a ghost. I do not think that anybody knows to this day exactly what happened there. This labourer was called Guðmundur. I think he was Jónsson, and was associated with Krossavík. He was a real muscle-man in build.

He was out walking when it happened. A published source says that he was going over Heiðarendi from Heiðarsel going north, and he saw that somebody was walking parallel to him all the time. My mother and my grandfather told me that when Guðmundur had got past Teigasel and had started on the last part of the trip, he became aware that the spook was in a hollow just before Teigará, just inside the land belonging to Teigasel. The spook came down the hollow which has since been called Draugslág ("Ghost's Hollow"). The ghost kept getting in Guðmundur's path almost all the way home. It ended with Guðmundur and the ghost fighting on the last part of the track. Guðmundur then staggered home with his clothes in a very bad state. His clothes were torn to pieces and his neck blue, very bruised. He was bed-ridden for the next few days. It may be added that according to my grandfather, Guðmundur was so afraid of the dark after that that for the rest of the winter he always had to be accompanied whenever he went out to look after the animals in the sheep house.)

The published source that Þorkell Björnsson refers to in his account must be *Ævisaga Eyjasels-Móra* by Halldór Pétursson. This book contains an account which is called "Glíma Guðmundar og Móra" ("The Wrestling of Guðmundur and Móri"). For the sake of context, I would like to give this account in full:

Guðmundur hét maður, Jónsson, Eyjólfssonar að Ekru. Hann var talinn tveggja manna maki og harðskeyttur að sama skapi. Margar eru sögur af svaðilförum Guðmundar, því að hann lét sér ekki allt fyrir brjósti brenna. Guðmundur var um skeið vinnumaður á Skeggjastöðum á Jökuldal. Þaðan skrapp hann til Seyðisfjarðar að vetrarlagi.

...Hann verður á heimleiðinni var við ókenndan förunaut við hlið sér er hann fer norður Tunguna (Hróarstungu). Þetta vakti Guðmundi geig og óhug, því að snáði þessi gerðist æ nærgöngulli, einkum þó fyrir heiðarendann og niður í Jökuldalinn. Inn Dalinn jókst svo ásókn þessi enn, og vildi þá náungi þessi kreppa Guðmund niður að Jökulsánni. Milli Teigasels og Skeggjastaða hófst orrustan fyrir alvöru. Gekk þá gestur þessi þvers og kruss fyrir Guðmund, svo að hann komst lítt áfram, og loks lagði fjandi þessi til atlögu við hann. Náungi þessi var í mórauðum fötum, mjög snjáðum. Á höfði bar hann hattkúf ljótan, og voru börðin skörðótt mjög. Guðmundur tók á móti af karlmennsku og hugðist reka djöful þennan undir sig, því að ekki sýndist þetta gerpimenni. En sigurinn reyndist ekki eins auðunninn og hann hugði. Hvar sem hann tók á drussa þessum, var hann sleipur og afsleppur, svo að hvergi fengust föst tök, og mjög var hann laus fyrir. Aftur á móti hafði hann Guðmund á loft og sóttist eftir að ná á honum hálstaki. Þannig áttust þeir við alla bæjarleiðina, og veitti ýmsum betur. Mundu þó fáir hafa viljað etja við Guðmund í slíkum ham. Lokasennan stóð heima við túnið á Skeggjastöðum. Neytti þá draugsi allra bragða, að Guðmundur næði ekki bænum. Guðmundur sá nú, að skammt mundi milli lífs og dauða. Fengi hann ekki náð bænum, mundi hér einn endir á verða, því að mjög var honum þá þorrinn þróttur. Færðist hann nú í aukana og er sem hamremmi grípi hann. Stundum finnst honum, að hann hafi djöfsa undir og ætlar þá að láta kné fylgja kviði, en í sömu andrá er óvættur þessi komin á bak honum og spennir greipar um háls hans. Tekur hann þá að formæla draugsa með svo kröftugum munnsöfnuði sem hann má og biður sjálfan djöfulinn að steikja hann á logandi teinum. Dró þá svo af náunga þessum, að Guðmundur gat losað krumlur hans af hálsi sér og gekk þá berserksgang með orðum og athöfnum.

Viðureign þeirra lauk síðan með því, að félaginn leystist upp í eldglæringar, og var sem af þeim legði ódaun mikinn. Komst Guðmundur við þetta inn fyrir túngarðinn og náði bænum. En svo var af honum dregið, að hann var vart viðmælandi lengi á eftir. Föt hans voru tætt og táin og svartir blettir á hálsi hans. Guðmundi sagðist svo frá, að það yrði sitt síðasta, ef djöfull sá réðist á sig aftur.[3]

(There was a man called Guðmundur Jónsson, the grandson of Eyjólfur of Ekra. He was considered to be the equal of two men in strength, and rough with it. There are many tales about Guðmundur's terrible journey, because there was little that he was frightened of. Guðmundur worked for a while as a labourer at Skeggjastaðir in the Jökuldalur valley. From there, he popped over to Seyðisfjörður one winter.

... he was on his way back home when he became aware of a

---

3   Halldór Pétursson 1962, 73-74.

strange travelling companion walking parallel to him as he went
north along Tunga (Hróarstunga). This gave Guðmundur a feeling
of both fear and dread, because this character was getting nearer
and nearer all the time, and especially towards the end of the heath
as they went down into Jökuldalur. In the Jökuldalur valley, this
bother went on getting worse, this chap trying to force Guðmundur into the Jökulsá river. The fight began for real somewhere
between Teigasel and Skeggjastaðir. The stranger kept crossing in
front of Guðmundur, preventing him from getting anywhere, and
eventually this demon attacked him. This chap was wearing tattered rust-brown clothes, and an ugly, shapeless hat with a very
ragged rim. Guðmundur received him like a man, and expected to
floor this devil immediately, because he did not seem to be much
of a fighter. However, winning did not turn out to be as easy as he
had expected. Wherever he took hold of this ruffian, he found him
slippery and loose, so that it was impossible to get a grip on him.
On the other hand, he had Guðmundur up in the air, and was trying to get him in a neck hold. That was how they fought all the
way towards the farm, and both seemed to be doing well. Few people would have wanted to challenge Guðmundur in the mood that
he was in now. The final showdown took place in the home field at
Skeggjastaðir. Then the spook tried all the tricks he knew in order
to prevent Guðmundur from reaching the farm. Guðmundur
could now see that it was going to be a matter of life and death. If
he did not reach the farm, there would be only one way in which
this could end, because his strength was running out. He now put
everything he had into it, and was like a man possessed. Sometimes he thought he had the devil beaten and was going to put an
end to it when he suddenly found this spirit on his back, tighten-
ing his grip about his throat. He then started cursing the spook in
the strongest language that he knew, even inviting the devil to
roast him on burning sticks. At that point, this chap seemed to
grow weaker, allowing Guðmundur to get his paws off his neck.
Guðmundur then went totally berserk in both words and in
action.

The fight ended with Guðmundur's opponent disappearing in
a shower of sparks which gave off a foul smell. Guðmundur then
got inside the home-field wall, and reached the farm. He was so
exhausted that it was a long time before he could really say much.
His clothes were tattered and torn, and he had black marks on his
neck. Guðmundur said that it would be his end if he got attacked
by that devil again.)

The third account of the aforementioned wrestling match with a ghost in which Guðmundur, the labourer at Skeggjastaðir, was supposed to have taken part can be found in *Austfirðingaþættir* by Gísli Helgason, which was published in 1949. This contains the tale of Guðmundur, the son of Björn and Aðalbjörg of Ekkjufell, and amongst other things, gives the following account:

Um það leyti, sem Aðalbjörg hætti búskap, fór Guðmundur í vinnumennsku. Var hann í nokkur ár vinnumaður hjá Jóni Magnússyni bónda á Skeggjastöðum á Dal... Þá var það einn laugardag laust fyrir göngur, að Guðmundur bað Jón húsbónda sinn að ljá sér hest um kvöldið út að Fossvöllum... Jón tók vel undir þetta, en kvaðst vona, að hann kæmi heim fyrir háttatíma á sunnudagskvöldið, og hét Guðmundur góðu um það. Fór hann út eftir og hafði með sér eitthvað af brennivíni, sem hann átti í fórum sínum... Síðara hluta sunnudagsins kom þangað Guðmundur Jónsson, sem þá bjó í Blöndugerði, og var allmikið drukkinn. Hann var mjög þreklegur maður og talinn vel sterkur, en óróagjarn við vín og vildi þá reyna krafta sína; þess utan var hann stilltur. Tók hann nú að stríða nafna sínum og ögra honum, en Guðmundur Björnsson fór undan í flæmingi og vildi leiða hjá sér illindi í lengstu lög, enda leið þá að kvöldi og orðið mál að halda heimleiðis, ef efna skyldi heitin við húsbóndann. Náði hann í hest sinn og hélt af stað heldur tómlega án þess að kveðja nafna sinn. Síðan reið hann fram og niður að brúnni á Jökulsá, en þegar hann nálgaðist hana, heyrði hann nafna senda sér tóninn og skora á sig að bíða, en renna eigi undan sem raggeit. Þegar yfir brúna kom, sté Guðmundur Björnsson af baki og lét nafna sinn vita, að hann væri ekkert smeykur við hann. Kom hinn þá yfir á eftir honum, og reyndu þeir með sér nokkrum sinnum; fór jafnan á sömu leið, að Guðmundur Jónsson laut í lægra haldi. Skildu þeir við það, og tók Guðmundur Björnsson hest sinn og reið inn eftir sem leið lá, en þegar hann var kominn inn á milli Gilja og Teigasels, heyrði hann enn til nafna síns, sem kom á eftir honum og kallaði, að hann rynni og þyrði ekki að bíða sín. "Víst skal nú bíða," kallaði Guðmundur Björnsson á móti, "og vilja hef ég nú að leika svo við þig, að þú eltir mig ekki lengra." Ekki er að orðlengja það, að þarna flugust þeir nafnar á allengi. Veitti Guðmundi Björnsyni jafnan betur og lék nafna sinn allharðlega, reif mjög af honum fötin og fór ómjúkum höndum um hann. Síðan tók hann hest sinn og náði allra síðustu háttum að Skeggjastöðum.

Guðmundur Jónsson kom aftur á móti ekki heim til sín fyrr en um fótaferð og var þá fremur illa til reika, föt hans rifin flest fyrir ofan mitti, en sums staðar var hann blár og blóðrísa. Kvaðst hann hafa glímt við draug alla nóttina, svo sem verksummerki sýndu, og er óhætt að segja að sú skýring hafi verið tekin góð og gild af æðimörgum í þá daga. - Hefur Guðmundur kunnað betur við að skýra ófarir sínar á þenna hátt en að segja hið sanna, enda átti hann alla sök á viðureign þessari. Hins vegar er óvíst, hvort Guðmundur Björnson hefði átt auðveldum sigri að fagna, ef nafni hans hefði verið lítið eða ekki ölvaður, því að talinn var hann mjög hraustur maður og hinn stilltasti utan víns.

Sögu þessa um viðskipti þeirra nafna sagði mér Magnús Sigbjörnsson á Akureyri, fyrrum bóndi á Hallgeirsstöðum og Ketilsstöðum í Jökulsárhlíð, en honum sagði Guðmundur Björnsson sjálfur. Kom Magnús til hans eitt sinn að Seli, er hann var á leið frá Seyðisfirði, og veitti honum brennivín. Guðmundur gekk þá með honum á leið og sagði honum frá þessum atburði...[4]

(At about the time that Aðalbjörg stopped farming, Guðmundur started working as a labourer. He spent several years working as a labourer for Jón Magnússon, the farmer at Skeggjastaðir in Dalur... One Saturday, a short time before the sheep were collected for the winter, Guðmundur asked his master Jón if he could borrow a horse to go out to Fossvellir for the evening... Jón took this request well, but said that he hoped that Guðmundur would be back before bedtime on Sunday evening. Guðmundur promised that he would be. He went out, and took with him a bottle of spirits that he had in his bag... On Sunday afternoon, a man named Guðmundur Jónsson who was then living at Blöndugerði arrived there (at Fossvellir). He was very drunk. He was a powerfully built man, and believed to be very strong, but he tended to get excitable when he drank, and at such times liked to show off his strength. Otherwise he was a very restrained man. He now started taunting his namesake, trying to work him up, but Guðmundur Björnsson was rather evasive, trying to avoid trouble for as long as was humanly possible. Otherwise, it was getting towards evening, and time to be heading back home if he was going to keep his promise to his master. He collected his horse and set off rather quietly, without saying goodbye to his namesake. He rode on, down towards the bridge over the Jökulsá river, but as he reached that he heard his namesake's voice, challenging him to wait rather than

---

4   Gísli Helgason 1949, 97; 102-104.

run away like a coward. When he had got over the river, Guð-mundur Björnsson dismounted and let his namesake know that he was not afraid of him. He then crossed the river after him and they had a few bouts, most of which ended in the same way: Guð-mundur Björnsson had the upper hand. They then parted, and Guðmundur Björnsson took his horse and rode on his way. But when he was between Gil and Teigasel, he heard his namesake once again, coming after him, calling out that he was running and did not dare to wait. "I'll certainly wait," called back Guð-mundur Björnsson, "and I am now quite ready to deal with you in such a way that you won't follow me any farther." There is no need to spin it out: these two namesakes now fought for a long time. Guðmundur Björnsson tended to give more than he received, and treated his namesake very roughly indeed, tearing many of his clothes off him, in general dealing with him in a very harsh man-ner. He then took his horse, and at last got back to Skeggjastaðir when the last people were going to bed.

Guðmundur Jónsson, on the other hand, did not get back home until people were getting up, and he was in a very sorry state. Most of his clothes above his waist were torn, and in some places he was bruised and bleeding. He said that he had been wrestling with a ghost all night just as his appearance seemed to suggest, and there is little question that this explanation was taken by many people at that time as being the truth. - Guðmundur felt that this was the best way to explain what had happened to him, and of course he was to blame for the fight taking place. On the other hand, it is questionable whether his namesake would have found it so easy to win if his namesake had been sober or only slightly drunk, because he was considered to be a very healthy man, and the most restrained of people when he was not drunk.

I was told this story of these two namesakes' dealings by Mag-nús Sigbjörnsson from Akureyri, who used to be a farmer at Hall-geirsstaðir and Ketilsstaðir in Jökulsárhlíð. He had been told of what happened by Guðmundur Björnsson himself. Magnús once came to Sel when he was on his way from Seyðisfjörður, and gave him some brennivín. Guðmundur then walked with him for a bit, and told him about what happened.)

The next step is to compare these three accounts. Guðmundur, the labourer at Skeggjastaðir in Jökuldalur, is referred to as "Jóns-son" in two of the sources (ÞB and HP) but as "Björnsson" in the third (GH). All of the accounts tell how Guðmundur was involved in a fight on the way home, two of them recounting how he had fought with a ghost (ÞB and HP), while the third says that the person who fought with Guðmundur informed others that he had fought with a ghost (GH). In all three accounts, the final battle is said to have taken place in the same area, that is to say between Teigasel and Skeggjastaðir, at a place later called Draugslág ("Ghost's Hollow": ÞB); close to the home field at Skeggjastaðir (HP), and between Gil and Teigasel (GH). Guðmundur's resulting condition is described in various ways: he was bedridden for the next few days (ÞB); he hardly spoke for a long time afterwards (HP); and he took his horse and rode home, while the person with whom he had fought returned home in a sorry state (GH).

There are certain key differences in the nature of these accounts. In two of them, it is stated outright that a supernatural occurrence had taken place.

"I do not think that anybody to this day knows exactly what happened there," writes Þorkell Björnsson, and in his conclusion, he adds that Guðmundur was frightened of the dark for the rest of that winter, and needed to be accompanied out to the lamb shed.

Halldór Pétursson's account places more emphasis on the supernatural, and bears many features of the archetypal ghost story. The ghost is introduced in the usual fashion, its description involving many characteristics found in similar ghost tales from earlier collections of folktales. A well-known motif is when the ghost tries to force Guðmundur into the Jökulsá river. Furthermore, the description of the wrestling itself has many parallels with earlier descriptions of people wrestling with ghosts. One innovation in Halldór Pétursson's account, however, is the way Guðmundur is said to have called on the devil in order to win his support. In earlier legends, people in similar difficulties usually call on God or a particular protecting saint. At the same time, the final motif of how the ghostly opponent disappeared in a foul-smelling shower of sparks is very common.

Gísli Helgason's account is different to the others in that it contains nothing supernatural. It tells simply of two drunken men getting into a brawl, the loser telling others that he had fought with a ghost. According to the writer, this was merely an excuse.

We can now examine the possible relationship between these

legends, and try to see what their origin might be. For this purpose, I mean to go over the accounts and examine the historical sources referred to in each case, as well as other reliable relevant material.

Guðmundur Jónsson is said to have been the grandson of Eyjólfur of Ekra (HP), and supposedly associated with Krossavík (ÞB). This seems to be the same person as the Guðmundur Jónsson referred to in *Ættir Austfirðinga* (2928), who was also the grandson of Eyjólfur of Ekra, and lived last at Krossavík. He married Guðrún Guðmundsdóttir in 1887, and they had four children, named Guðmundur, Guðbjörg, Jóhanna and Jón.[5]

Two of the accounts (ÞB and GH) state that Guðmundur was a labourer for Jón Magnússon, the farmer who lived at Skeggjastaðir between 1874 and 1916.[6] The list of parishioners for the parish of Hofteigur for that period only once mentions a labourer named Guðmundur Jónsson, but he was only 20 years old in 1902. On the other hand, we do find a man named Guðmundur Björnsson listed as a labourer at Skeggjastaðir between the years 1889-1891, and he is said to have been 28 years old in 1891.[7] According to the list of parishioners for the parish of Kirkjubær for 1891, Guðmundur Jónsson is registered as having been a farmer at Blöndugerði, along with his wife Guðrún Guðmundsdóttir and their two children, Guðmundur and Guðbjörg. At that time, Guðmundur is said to have been 29 years old.[8] There is no question that this is the Guðmundur who later lived at Krossavík and was the son of Jón Eyjólfsson of Ekra.

In the light of the information given above, it seems most likely that the real fight that took place between Guðmundur Björnsson and Guðmundur Jónsson formed the basis for all of the forms of the story under discussion. Guðmundur Jónsson was probably the person who started off the story to do with wrestling a ghost, and one of his listeners was probably aware that Guðmundur Björnsson, the labourer at Skeggjastaðir had supposedly been involved in a fight with an evil-minded opponent at around the same time. The names of the two Guðmundurs probably helped cause the confusion

---

5   Einar Jónsson 1953, 208; 292-293.
6   *Sveitir og jarðir í Múlaþingi* I 1974, 305.
7   *Sóknarmannatal Hofteigssóknar* 1891.
8   *Sóknarmannatal Kirkjubæjar* 1891.

of figures in the oral transmission of the story so that eventually the Guðmundur who wrestled with a ghost became "Guðmundur *Jóns-son*, the labourer at Skeggjastaðir" (HP). The fact that there was a man named Guðmundur Jónsson who worked for one year at Skeggjastaðir after the turn of the century may well have had some influence. Þorkell Björnsson is not certain about the name of Guðmundur's father, but he appears to support the earlier noted fact or that which appears in Halldór Pétursson's account when he states that he "thinks" that Guðmundur the labourer was the son of Jón.

If these three accounts are to be graded according to the classification system used in the study of folk legends, it can be concluded that the only real legend is that given by Gísli Helgason. This is a *memorat*, based on the memory of an event, which Guðmundur Björnsson told Magnús Sigbjörnsson, and Gísli of Skógargerði recorded from Magnús. Þorkell's account is a legend of belief, a *fabulat*, which Þorkell heard from his mother Guðríður and his grandfather Jón Magnússon. This account is further away from the original events than Gísli's record, and contains no words from Guðmundur the labourer himself. The basis of Halldór Pétursson's account is also a legend of belief, but it is even further away from the actual events that took place than Þorkell's version. Admittedly Halldór's version still contains certain characteristics typical of oral legends in that references are made to named individuals and places, but at the same time the account has adopted various fantastic elements from traditional ghost stories which cause it to be classed as standing on the borderline between a factual legend and an imaginative folk tale.

I mentioned earlier that with regard to the folktales and legends from earlier times concerning wrestling with a ghost it is often difficult to decide whether they were inspired by a particular realistic or unrealistic event. There is little comparative material to be found anywhere in the older folk legends and tales, and usually the living person who took part in the wrestling was alone in those accounts.[9] On the other hand, the above examination of these three legends recorded in eastern Iceland has the benefit of further information,

---

9   See above pp. 143 ff.; 155-156.

and thus sheds light on how such wrestling legends and tales might have been formed in the oral tradition.

The aforementioned three versions of a legend to do with wrestling with a ghost that was supposed to have taken place just outside Skeggjastaðir in Jökuldalur clearly have great value as comparative material that can be used when evaluating the formation of earlier tales to do with this same particular phenomenon. I felt it fitting to publish this brief examination alongside the republication of my earlier article on the same subject in order to allow readers to have the benefit of a more recent study of comparative material.

Those amateur historians and collectors of local lore from the east of Iceland who recorded and preserved these legends in their various forms for posterity deserve our eternal gratitude.

Translated by Terry Gunnell

Ágrip

Draugurinn sem glímdi við Guðmund

Í RITGERÐINNI „Draugurinn sem glímdi við Guðmund", eru teknar til athugunar þrjár frásagnir af glímu við draug sem allar eru skrásettar á Austurlandi um og eftir miðja tuttugustu öld. Atvikin sem greint er frá eru öll sögð hafa gerst á svipuðum tíma, laust fyrir síðustu aldamót, og á sömu slóðum, skammt fyrir utan Skeggjastaði á Jökuldal.

Þorkell Björnsson hefur það eftir afa sínum, Jóni Magnússyni, bónda á Skeggjastöðum, og móður sinni, Guðríði Jónsdóttur, að vinnumaður hjá Jóni, Guðmundur, sem Þorkell hyggur að hafi verið Jónsson, hafi eitt sinn lent í "hörkuáflogum við draug" og verið miður sín um nokkurn tíma eftir það. Þorkell telur ótrúlegt að unnt verði að skýra hvað þarna gerðist. Saga Þorkels um glímuna við drauginn er skráð 1981.

Árið 1962 birti Halldór Pétursson frásögn af glímu við draug á ssömu slóðum, sem hann kvað Guðmund Jónsson, vinnumann á Skeggjastöðum,

---

The Ghost that wrestled with Guðmundur was originally published as part of another paper in *Indriðabók. Greinar af sama meiði helgaðar Indriða Gíslasyni sjötugum*, 1998. It is published here with minor alterations.

hafa þreytt við Eyjasels-Móra. Lýsingin á glímunni og atgangi öllum er
með miklum ólíkindablæ í þessari frásögn og ber mjög svip af eldri lýsingum hliðstæðra átaka í fornritum og þjóðsögum.

Gísli Helgason í Skógargerði birti þætti af ýmsum Austfirðingum árið
1949. Þar segir frá Guðmundi Björnssyni frá Ekkjufelli sem var vinnumaður hjá Jóni á Skeggjastöðum um 1890. Segir Gísli sögu af því eftir
góðum heimildum, er Guðmundur Björnsson var á leið frá Fossvöllum til
Skeggjastaða að kvöldlagi og nokkuð við skál, er nafni hans, Guðmundur
Jónsson i Blöndugerði, elti hann og margmanaði til átaka. Glímdu þeir
nafnar nokkrum sinnum og hafði Guðmundur Björnsson jafnan betur.
Guðmundur Jónsson kom heim til sín í Blöndugerði, tættur og rifinn
undir morgun og kvaðst hafa flogist á við draug alla nóttina.

Í ritgerðinni eru leiddar líkur að því að þessi átök þeirra nafnanna hafi
verið kveikjan að sögunni um glímu Guðmundar vinnumanns á Skeggjastöðum við drauginn.

Bibliography

Unpublished sources

The Dictionary of the Arnemagnean Institute in Copenhagen
Sóknarmannatal Hofteigssóknar 1876-1920
Sóknarmannatal Kirkjubæjarsóknar 1890-1900

Published sources

Adam of Bremen 1917: *Gesta Hammaburgensis Ecclesiæ Pontificum.* Hrgg. B. Schmeidler. Hannover and Leipzig.

Alexanders saga 1925. Ed. Finnur Jónsson.. Khvn.

Almqvist, Bo 1967: "Nid". *KLNM* XII, 295-299. Rvík.

The Anglo-Saxon Chronicle 1953 (1978). Translated with an introduction by G. N. Garmonsway. London.

Austfirðinga sǫgur 1950. Ed. Jón Jóhannesson. *ÍF* XI. Rvík.

Ágrip af Nóregskonunga sǫgum 1984. Ed. Bjarni Einarsson. *ÍF* XXIX, 1-54. Rvík.

Árni Óla 1968: *Álög og bannhelgi.* Rvík.

Baetke, Walter 1973: *Kleine Schriften.* Weimar.

Bjarni Aðalbjarnarson 1936: "Om de norske konger sagaer". *NVAOS,* Kl. II, No. 4. Oslo.

Björn M. Ólsen 1900: *Um kristnitökuna árið 1000 og tildrög hennar.* Rvík.

Björn Sigfússon 1959: "Eyrbyggja saga". *KLNM* IV, 104. Rvík.

Björn Sigfússon 1960: "Grettis saga Ásmundarsonar". *KLNM* V, 460-461. Rvík.

Björn Þorsteinsson 1966: *Ný Íslandssaga.* Rvík.

Björn K. Þórólfsson 1934: *Rímur fyrir 1600.* Khvn.

The Book of Settlements 1972. Trans. by Hermann Pálsson and Paul Edwards. Manitoba.

Bókfræði Hrafnkels sögu Freysgoða 1993. Ed. Kristján Jóhann Jónsson. Egilsstaðir.

Brown, Ursula, 1952, ed. *Þorgils saga ok Haflíða.* Oxford.

Cleasby, Richard, and Vigfússon, Guðbrandur 1975: *An Icelandic English Dictionary.* 2nd ed. with supplement by W. Craigie. Oxford.

The Complete Sagas of Icelanders I-V. 1997. Ed. Viðar Hreinsson et al. Trans. Robert Cook et al. Rvík.

Cumont, Franz, 1956: *The Mysteries of Mithra.* New York.

David, Rosalie, 1980: "Egypt", in Cavendish, Richard, ed.: *Mythology. An Illustrated Encyclopedia,* 96-109. London.

Bibliography

Davidson, H. R. Ellis 1981: "The Restless Dead: An Icelandic Ghost Story". *The Folklore of Ghosts,* 155-175. Ed. H. R. E. Davidson, and W. M. S. Russell. London.

Dillmann, François-Xavier 1997: "Kring de rituella gästabuden i fornskandinavisk religion". *Uppsalakulten och Adam av Bremen.* Ed. Anders Hultgård. Uppsala.

Diplomatarium Islandicum 1857 ff. Vol. I ff. Khvn and Rvík.

Droplaugarsona saga 1950. Ed. Jón Jóhannesson. *ÍF* XI, 135-180. Rvík.

Dumézil, Georges 1973: *Gods of the Ancient Northmen.* Berkeley.

Edda 1987 = Snorri Sturluson: *Edda.* Trans. Anthony Faulkes. London.

Edda 1962 (1983). *Die Lieder des Codex Regius.* Ed. Gustav Neckel and Hans Kuhn. Heidelberg.

The Poetic Edda 1962. Trans. Lee M. Hollander. Austin, Texas.

Eddadigte I 1962. *Vǫluspá. Hávamál.* Ed. Jón Helgason. *Nordisk filologi.* Khvn.

Eddadigte II 1962. *Gudedigte.* Ed. Jón Helgason. *Nordisk filologi.* Khvn.

Eddukvæði 1968. Ed. Ólafur Briem. Rvík.

Egils saga einhenda ok Ásmundar berserkjabana 1944. *FN* III, 153-189. Rvík.

Egils saga Skalla-Grímssonar 1933. Ed. Sigurður Nordal. *ÍF* II. Rvík.

Egils saga 1960. Trans. Gwyn Jones. New York.

Egils saga 1976. Trans. Hermann Pálsson and Paul Edwards. Harmondsworth.

Einar Jónsson 1953: *Ættir Austfirðinga.* Vol. 1. Rvík.

Einar G. Pétursson 1997: "Þjóðtrú á Íslandi". *Frændafundur* 2, 59-71. Ed. Turið Sigurðardóttir and Magnús Snædal. Tórshavn.

Einar Ól. Sveinsson 1959: "Fornaldarsögur Norðurlanda", *KLNM* IV, 499-507. Rvík.

Einar Ól. Sveinsson 1968: "Eyrbyggja sagas kilder". *Scripta Islandica* 19, 3-18. Uppsala.

Eliade, Mircea 1973: "Myth in the Nineteenth and Twentieth Centuries". *Dictionary of the History of Ideas* III. Ed. Philip H. Wiener, 306-318. New York.

Eliade, Mircea, 1983: *Patterns in Comparative Religion.* London.

Ellehøj, Svend, 1965: "Studier over den ældste norrøne historieskrivning". *Bibliotheca Arnamagnæana* Vol. XXVI. Khvn.

Eyrbyggja saga 1935. Ed. Einar Ól. Sveinsson. *ÍF* IV, 1-184. Rvík.

Fagrskinna - Nóregs konunga tal 1984. Ed. Bjarni Einarsson. *ÍF* XXIX, 55-373. Rvík.

Finnur Jónsson 1898: "Hofalýsingar í fornsögum og goðalíkneski". *Árbók Hins íslenzka fornleifafélags,* Rvík.

Finnur Jónsson, ed. *Den norsk-islandske skjaldediktning.* A: 1-2. B: 1-2. Khvn and Kria 1908-1915.

Flateyjarbók I-III 1944-1945. Ed. Sigurður Nordal. Rvík.

Folklore of Ghosts, see Davidson.

Foote, Peter G. 1975: "Observations on the 'syncretism' in early Icelandic Christianity". *Árbók Vísindafélags Íslendinga* 1974. Rvík.

Bibliography

Foote, Peter G. 1982: "Under the Cloak". *Arv* 1979, 155-159. Uppsala.

Foote, Peter G. 1984: *Aurvandilstá. Norse Studies.* Odense.

Foote, Peter G. 1984: "Sagnaskemmtun: Reykjahólar 1119". In Foote, Peter G.: *Aurvandilstá. Norse Studies,* 65-83. Odense.

Fornaldarsögur Norðurlanda II-III 1944. Ed. Guðni Jónsson and Bjarni Vilhjálms-son. Rvík.

Gísla saga Súrssonar 1943. Ed. Björn Karel Þórólfsson. *ÍF* VI, 1-118. Rvík

Gísli Helgason í Skógargerði 1949: *Austfirðingaþættir.* Akureyri.

Grágás I-II, *Konungsbók,* 1974. A Photographed Reproduction of Vilhjálmur Finsen's edition 1852. Odense.

Grágás, Staðarhólsbók, 1974. A Photographed Reproduction of Vilhjálmur Finsen's edition 1879. Odense.

Gráskinna hin meiri I 1962. Ed. Sigurður Nordal and Þórbergur Þórðarson. Rvík.

Grettis saga Ásmundarsonar 1936. Ed. Guðni Jónsson. *ÍF* VII, 1-290. Rvík.

Griplur III. *Rímnasafn* I 1905-1912. Ed. Finnur Jónsson. Khvn.

Guðmundur Finnbogason 1929: "Lífsskoðun Hávamála og Aristóteles". *Skírnir,* 84-102. Rvík.

Guðrún Bjartmarsdóttir 1982: "Ljúflingar og fleira fólk". *Tímarit Máls og menningar,* 319-336. Rvík.

Guðrún Nordal 1992: "Freyr fífldur". *Skírnir,* 271-294.

Guðrún Nordal 1995: "Trúskipti og písl í Hrafnkels sögu". *Gripla* IX, 97-114. Rvík.

Gunnell, Terry 1995: *The Origins of Drama in Scandinavia.* Woodbridge.

Halldór Pétursson 1962: *Ævisaga Eyjasels-Móra.* Rvík.

Halvorsen, E. F. 1959: "Fagrskinna". *KLNM* IV, 139-140. Rvík.

Halvorsen, E. F. 1962: "Hræsvelgr and Jotner". *KLNM* VII, 30-31 and 693-697. Rvík.

Halvorsen, E. F. 1976: "Þorri". *KLNM* XX, 395-397. Rvík.

Harðar saga Grímkelssonar eða Hólmverja saga 1991. Ed. Þórhallur Vilmundarson. *ÍF* XIII, 1-97. Rvík.

Harðar saga og Hólmverja 1987. *Íslendinga sögur og þættir* II, 1253-1299. Ed. Bragi Halldórsson, Jón Torfason, Sverrir Tómasson and Örnólfur Thorsson. Rvík.

Harris, Joseph, 1985: "Eddic Poetry", in *Old Norse-Icelandic Literature, Islandica* XLV, 68-156. Ed. Carol J. Clover and John Lindow. Ithaca and London.

Heiðarvíga saga 1934. Ed. Sigurður Nordal and Guðni Jónsson. *ÍF* III, 213-328.

Historia Norwegiæ 1880. Ed. Gustav Storm. *Monumenta Historica Norwegiæ,* 69-124. Kria.

Hofmann, Dietrich 1976: "Hrafnkels und Hallfreðs Traum". *Skandinavistik* 1, 19-36.

Holbek, B. and Piø, I. 1979: *Fabeldyr og sagnfolk.* Khvn.

Holm-Olsen, L., 1961: "Hákonarmál". *KLNM* VI, 50-51. Rvík.

Holtsmark, Anne 1933: "Vitazgjafi". *Maal og minne,* 111-133. Oslo.

Holtsmark, Anne, 1949: "Myten om Idun og Tjatse i Tjodolvs Haustlöng". *ANF* 64, 1-73. Lund.

Bibliography

Holtsmark, Anne, 1958: "Edda den yngre". *KLNM* III, 475-480. Rvík.

Holtsmark, Anne, 1960: "Gói". *KLNM* V, 366-368. Rvík.

Holtsmark, Anne, 1961: "Historia Norwegiæ". *KLNM* VI, 585-587. Rvík.

Hrafnkels saga Freysgoða 1950. Ed. Jón Jóhannesson. *ÍF* XI, 95-133. Rvík.

Hugtök og heiti í bókmenntafræði 1983. Ed. Jakob Benediktsson. Rvík.

Höfler, O. 1959: "Der Sakralcharakter des germanischen Königtums". *The Sacral Kingship*, 664-701. Leiden.

Íslendingabók. Landnámabók 1968. Ed. Jakob Benediktson. *ÍF* I. Rvík.

Íslenzkir sagnaþættir og þjóðsögur XII 1957. Ed. Guðni Jónsson. Rvík.

Jakob Benediktsson 1976: "Þorgils saga ok Hafliða". *KLNM* XX, 384-385. Rvík.

Jesch, Judith 1984: "Hromundr Gripsson revisited". *Scandinavistik* 14, 89-105.

Jón Hnefill Aðalsteinsson 1978: *Under the Cloak*. Uppsala.

Jón Hnefill Aðalsteinsson 1985a: "Blót and þing. The Function of the Tenth-Century *goði*." *Temenos* 21, 23-38. Helsinki.

Jón Hnefill Aðalsteinsson 1985b: *Þjóðtrú og þjóðfræði*. Rvík.

Jón Hnefill Aðalsteinsson 1986: *Eiður að baugi og hinn almáttki áss*. Rvík.

Jón Hnefill Aðalsteinsson 1989: "Þjóðsögur og sagnir". *Íslensk þjóðmenning* VII, ed. Frosti F. Jóhannsson, 228-290. Summary. Rvík.

Jón Hnefill Aðalsteinsson 1991: "Íslenski skólinn". *Skírnir*, 103-129. Rvík.

Jón Hnefill Aðalsteinsson 1992: "Freysminni í fornsögum". *Íslensk félagsrit* 2-4, 1990-1992. Rvík.

Jón Hnefill Aðalsteinsson 1997a: *Blót í norrænum sið. Rýnt í forn trúarbrögð með þjóðfræðilegri aðferð*. Rvík.

Jón Hnefill Aðalsteinsson 1997b: "Freyfaxahamarr". *Skáldakaparmál* 4, 238-253. Rvík.

Jón Hnefill Aðalsteinsson 1998: "Þjóðfræði á Austurlandi". *Indriðabók. Greinar af sama meiði helgaðar Indriða Gíslasyni sjötugum*, 357-370. Rvík.

Jón Árnason 1956-1961: *Íslenzkar þjóðsögur og ævintýri* I-VI. Ed. Árni Böðvarsson and Bjarni Vilhjálmsson. Rvík.

Jón Helgason 1953: "Norges og Islands digtning". *Nordisk kultur* VIII B, 3-179. Khvn.

Jón Jóhannesson 1956: *Íslendingasaga I. Þjóðveldisöld*. Rvík.

Jónas Kristjánsson 1978: "Bókmenntasaga". Sigurður Líndal, ed.: *Saga Íslands* III, 261-350.

Kjalnesinga saga 1959. Ed. Jóhannes Halldórsson. *ÍF* XIV, 1-44. Rvík.

Kulturhistorisk leksikon for nordisk middelalder 1956-1978. Vols. I-XXII. Rvík.

Landnámabók 1968. Jakob Benediktsson gaf út. Rvík. *ÍF* I.

Laxdæla saga 1934. Ed. Einar Ól. Sveinsson. *ÍF* V, 1-248. Rvík.

Laws of Early Iceland 1980. *Grágás* I. Trans. Andrew Dennis, Peter Foote, and Richard Perkins. London.

Liestøl, Knut 1946: "Tradisjonen i Hrafnkels saga Freysgoda". *Arv*, 94-110. Uppsala.

Lindow, John 1979: "Ritual Behavior at the Conversion of Iceland". *Ethnologia Scandinavica*, 178-179. Lund.

Bibliography

Lindow, John 1985: "Mythology and Mythography". In *Old Norse-Icelandic Literature, Islandica* XLV, 21-67. Ed. Carol J. Clover and John Lindow. Ithaca and London.

Ljungberg, Helge 1938: *Den nordiska religionen och kristendomen*. Uppsala.

Magnús Gestsson 1973: *Úr vesturbyggðum Barðastrandarsýslu*. Hafnarfjörður.

Magnús Már Lárusson 1958: "Íslenzkar mælieiningar". *Skírnir*, 208-245. Rvík.

Magnús Stefánsson 1975: "Kirkjuvald eflist". Sigurður Líndal, ed.: *Saga Íslands* II, 57-144. Rvík.

Martin, John Stanley 1981: "Ár vas alda". *Speculum Norrænum*, 357-369. Ed. Ursula Dronke, Guðrún P. Helgadóttir, Gerd Wolfgang Weber and Hans Bekker-Nielsen. Odense.

Maurer, Konrad 1852: *Die Entstehung des Isländischen Staates und seiner Verfassung*. München.

McTurk, R. W. 1976: "Sacral Kingship in Ancient Scandinavia. A Review of some Recent Writings". *Saga-Book* XIX, 139-169. London.

Meissner, Rudolf 1917: "Ganga til fréttar". *Zeitschrift des Vereins für Volkskunde* 27, 1-13. Berlin.

Meulengracht-Sørenen, Preben: "Murder in marital bed. An attempt at understanding a crucial scene in Gísla saga". *Structure and Meaning in Old Norse Literature. New Approaches to Textual Analysis and Literary Criticism*. Ed. John Lindow, Lars Lönnroth, and Gerd Wolfgang Weber, 235-263. Odense.

Mythology 1980. Ed. Richard Cavendish. London.

Nørlund, Poul, 1972: *Fornar byggðir á hjara heims*. Trans. Kristján Eldjárn. Rvík.

The Poetic Edda 1962. Trans. Lee M. Hollander. Austin, Texas.

"Oddaverja þáttr" 1953. *Byskupa sögur*, 131-154. Ed. Guðni Jónsson. Rvík.

The Odyssey of Homer 1903. Done into English by S. H. Butcher and A. Lang. London.

The Odyssey 1961. Trans. Robert Fitzgerald. London.

Odysseifskviða 1973. Trans. Sveinbjörn Egilsson. Ed. Kristinn Ármannsson and Jón Gíslason. Rvík.

Olsen, Magnus 1909: "Fra gammelnorsk myte og kultus". *Maal og minne*, 17-36. Oslo.

Olsen, Magnus 1934: "Þundarbenda". *Maal og minne*, 92-97. Oslo.

Olsen, Olof 1966: *Hørg, hov og kirke*. Khvn.

Opuscula. Vol. I 1960. Khvn.

Ólafur Lárusson 1958: *Lög og saga*. Rvík.

Ólafur Lárusson 1960: "Goði og goðorð". *KLNM* V, 363-366. Rvík.

Óskar Halldórsson 1976: *Uppruni og þema Hrafnkels sögu*. Rvík.

Óskar Halldórsson 1982: "Tröllasaga Bárðdæla og Grettluhöfundur". *Skírnir*, 5-36. Rvík.

Plummer, C. 1892-1899: *Two of the Saxon Chronicles* 876. Oxford.

Rímnasafn I, see *Griplur* III

Rooth, Anna Birgitta, 1961: *Loki in Scandinavian Mythology*. Lund.

Rooth, Anna Birgitta, 1982: *Öskubuska í austri og vestri.* Trans. into Icelandic by Svava Jakobsdóttir and Jón Hnefill Aðalsteinsson. Rvík.

Saga Íslands I 1974. Ed. Sigurður Líndal. Rvík.

Saga Íslands II 1975. Ed. Sigurður Líndal. Rvík.

Saga Íslands III 1978. Ed. Sigurður Líndal. Rvík.

Saxo Grammaticus 1979: *History of the Danes.* Volume I. English Text. Trans. Peter Fisher. Ed. Hilda Ellis Davidson. Cambridge.

Saxo Grammaticus 1980: *History of the Danes.* Volume II. Commentary. Hilda Ellis Davidson and Peter Fisher. Cambridge.

Saxo Grammaticus 1985: *Danmarks Krønike.* Trans. Fr. Winkel Horn. Khvn.

Saxonis Grammatici 1859: *Historia Danica.* Ed. Petrus Erasmus Müller and Johannes Matthias Velschow. Vol. I. Havniæ.

von See, Klaus, 1981: "Das Problem der mündlichen Erzählprosa im Altnordischen". *Scandinavistik* 11, 91-95.

von Sydow, C. W. 1919: "Jättarna i mytologi och folktro". *Folkminnen och Folktankar* 6, 52-96.

Sigfús Sigfússon 1982: *Íslenskar þjóðsögur og sagnir* II. Ed. Óskar Halldórsson. Rvík.

Sigurður Nordal 1940: "Hrafnkatla". *Studia Islandica* 7. Rvík.

Sigurður Nordal 1942: *Íslenzk menning* I. Rvík.

Sigurður Nordal 1952: *Völuspá.* 2nd ed. Rvík.

Sigurður Nordal 1953: "Sagalitteraturen". *NK* VIII B, 180-273. Khvn.

Sigurður Nordal 1972: *Þjóðsagnabókin* II. Rvík.

Sigurður Nordal 1973: *Snorri Sturluson.* 2nd ed. Rvík.

Símon Jóh. Ágústsson 1949: *Álitamál.* Rvík.

Snorra-Edda 1935 = *Edda Snorra Sturlusonar.* Ed. Guðni Jónsson. Rvík.

Snorri, átta alda minning 1979. Sögufélag. Rvík.

Snorri Sturluson 1931: *Edda.* Ed. Finnur Jónsson. Khvn.

Snorri Sturluson 1987. *Edda.* Ed. and trans. Antony Faulkes. London.

Snorri Sturluson 1941: *Heimskringla* I. Ed. Bjarni Aðalbjarnarson. *ÍF* XXVI. Rvík.

"Sonatorrek", see *Egils saga Skalla-Grímssonar* 1933, 246-256.

Steinsland, Gro: *Det hellige bryllup og norrøn kongeideologi.* Oslo 1991.

Storm, Gustav, 1880. Ed. *Monmenta Historica Norwegiæ.* Kria.

Ström, Å. V., 1959: "The King God and his Connection with Sacrifice in Old Norse Religion". *The Sacral Kingship*, 702-715. Leiden.

Strömbäck, Dag 1935: *Sejd.* Lund.

Strömbäck, Dag 1970: *Folklore and Filologi.* Uppsala.

Strömbäck, Dag 1975: *The Conversion of Iceland.* Trans. and annotated by Peter G. Foote. London.

Sturlunga saga I-II 1906-1911. Ed. Kristian Kålund. Khvn.

Sturlunga saga I 1946. Ed. Jón Jóhannesson, Magnús Finnbogason and Kristján Eldjárn. Rvík.

Bibliography

Svava Jakobsdóttir 1988: "Gunnlöð og hinn dýri mjöður". *Skírnir*, 215-245. Rvík.

Sveitir og jarðir í Múlaþingi 1974. Vol. I. Egilsstaðir

Svenska folksagor 1981. Andra bandet. Södertälje.

Sæmundar-Edda. *Eddukvæði* 1926. Ed. Finnur Jónsson. Rvík.

Tacitus, Cornelius 1928: *Germanía*. Trans. Páll Sveinsson. Rvík.

Turville-Petre, Gabriel 1953 (1975): *Origins of Icelandic Literature*. Oxford.

Turville-Petre, Gabriel 1964: *Myth and Religion of the North*. London.

Turville-Petre, Gabriel 1976: *Scaldic Poetry*. Oxford.

Ulset, Tor 1983: *Det genetiske forholdet mellom Ágrip, Historia Norwegiæ og Historia de antiquitate regum Norwagiensium*. Oslo.

Úlfar Bragason, ed. 1992: "Snorrastefna" *Rit Stofnunar Sigurðar Nordals* 1. Rvík.

Vafþrúðnismál 1988. Ed. Tim William Machan. Durham Medieval Texts, 6. Durham.

Valdimar Tr. Hafstein 1995: *Hjólaskóflur og huldufólk*. B. A. thesis in Landsbókasafn/Háskólabókasafn. (Unpublished).

Vatnsdæla saga 1939. Ed. Einar Ól. Sveinsson. ÍF VIII, 1-131. Rvík.

Vestfirzkar sagnir III 1946. Ed. Arngrímur Fr. Bjarnason. Rvík.

Vésteinn Ólason 1983: "Íslendingasögur". Jakob Benediktsson, ed.: *Hugtök og heiti í bókmenntafræði*.

Vésteinn Ólason 1994: "Morð í rekkju hjóna". *Sagnaþing, helgað Jónasi Kristjánssyni sjötugum*, 823-828. Rvík.

Víga-Glúms saga 1956. Ed. Jónas Kristjánsson. ÍF IX, 1-98. Rvík.

de Vries, Jan 1956-1957: *Altgermanische Religionsgeschichte* I-II. Berlin.

Weber, Gerd Wolfgang 1987: "Intelligera historiam. Typological perspectives of Nordic prehistory (in Snorri, Saxo. Widukind and others)". Ed. Kirsten Hastrup and Preben Meulengracht Sørensen. *Tradition og historieskrivning*, 95-141. *Acta Jutlandica* LXXIII: 2. Århus.

Weber, Gerd Wolfgang 1994: (review of) Úlfar Bragason, ed. Snorrastefna Rit Stofnunar Sigurðar Nordals 1. Rvík 1992. *Alvíssmál*, 121-128. Berlin.

Þorgils saga ok Hafliða 1952. Ed. Ursula Brown. Oxford.

Þorkell Björnsson frá Hnefilsdal 1981: *Af Jökuldalsmönnum og fleira fólki*. Rvík.

Ævi Snorra goða 1935. Ed. Einar Ól. Sveinsson. ÍF IV, 185-6. Rvík.

Abbreviations

ANF = *Arkiv för nordisk filologi*
DI = *Diplomatarium Islandicum.*
FN = *Fornaldarsögur Norðurlanda.*
GH = Gísli Helgason
Grg = *Grágás* I (a-b)-II, ed. Vilhjálmur Finsen, Khvn 1852-79.
HP = Halldór Pétursson
IAHR = International Association for the History of Religion.
ÍF = *Íslenzk fornrit.* 1933- (in progress).
ÍF I = *Íslendingabók. Landnámabók.*
ÍF II = *Egils saga Skalla-Grímssonar.*
ÍF III = *Heiðarvíga saga.*
ÍF IV = *Eyrbyggja saga. Ævi Snorra goða.*
ÍF V = *Laxdæla saga.*
ÍF VI = *Gísla saga Súrssonar.*
ÍF VII = *Grettis saga.*
ÍF VIII = *Vatnsdæla saga.*
ÍF IX = *Víga-Glúms saga* = *Glúma.*
ÍF XI = *Austfirðinga sǫgur: Hrafnkels saga Freysgoða* = *Hrafnkatla;*
    Droplaugarsona saga.
ÍF XII = *Njáls saga* = *Njála.*
ÍF XIII = *Harðar saga Grímkelssonar eða Hólmverja saga.*
ÍF XIV = *Kjalnesinga saga.*
ÍF XXVI = *Heimskringla I: Hákonar saga góða.*
ÍF XXIX = *Ágrip af Nóregskonunga sǫgum; Fagrskinna - Nóregs konunga tal.*
Khvn = København = Copenhagen.
KLNM = *Kulturhistorisk leksikon for nordisk middelalder*
    I-XXII. Rvík 1956-1978
Kria = Kristiania = Oslo.
NK = *Nordisk kultur*
NVAOS = *Det norske videnskabs-akademi i Oslos avhandlinger*
Rvík = Reykjavík
Sn.E. = *Snorra-Edda* = Snorri Sturluson: *Edda.*
ÞB = Þorkell Björnsson

182

Index